LIVE
THE
WORK
YOU
LOVE

LIVE THE WORK YOU LOVE

Creating your business legacy

PETER HYSON

Author: Peter Hyson
Published by The Write Factor

Copyright © 2016 by Peter Hyson
First Edition, 2016
Published in the UK by The Write Factor – www.thewritefactor.co.uk

Printed in the United Kingdom

10 9 8 7 6 5 4 3 2 1

DEDICATION

For HILARY ROWLAND whose support and encouragement, wisdom, knowledge and experience have immeasurably enriched not only the text of the book, but also my own life. She has challenged my thinking, helped broaden and deepen my understanding – and done so with joy. All this she has made possible, and I am eternally grateful.

ACKNOWLEDGEMENTS

Many people have contributed to the writing of this book. Some have been absorbed unconsciously over the years. More consciously I'm especially grateful to my Editor LORNA HOWARTH and her team at The Write Factor whose eye for detail and commitment to getting the best possible book has improved it so much.

ANDREW, LORD STONE OF BLACKHEATH; MIKE JOHNSON, formerly Global Head of Castrol at BP; and NEAL GANDHI, Investor, Philanthropist, Chairman of Farmflo, Questers Group, Rainmaker Foundation, The Green Marine & The Headshot Guy - who kindly gave time to tell me their stories with honesty and good humour for the Case Studies.

MATTHEW BAGWELL, Managing Director of naked Communications, contributed wise insights and advice at key moments.

GINA HAYDEN, CEO, Sphere Consulting provided personal encouragement, intellectual stimulation and numerous invaluable contacts.

And each of the following who kindly looked at the book and gave support and encouragement: GAUTAM BHUSHAN: Managing Partner, LearnTalent, Delhi, India.; TONY BURY: ROB CROSS, HR Director, UK & Ireland, SIG;

PRABHU GUPTARA: Advisory Board Member, New Global Markets, UK; Distinguished Professor of Global Business, William Carey University, India; formerly Director, Wolfsberg/UBS, Switzerland; PHIL JESSON: author *Piranhas in the Bidet — a snappy guide to better partnerships with your customers, your people and yourself*; CAROLINE LUKENSMYER: Founder & President, AmericaSpeaks/Global Voices; Executive Director, National Institute for Civil Discourse, Arizona, USA; GLADEANA MCMAHON: International author; Editorial Board, Coaching at Work; MD Gladeana McMahon; ANDREW MORRIS: formerly CEO, The Academy for Chief Executives; Non-exec Director, Business Design Centre; formerly Chair Brand Events; CEO, National Exhibition Centre; CEO Earls Court & Olympia; SUDHAKAR RAM, Group CEO and Managing Director at Mastek Ltd; CINDY WIGGLESWORTH: Author, SQ21: The Twenty-One Skills of Spiritual Intelligence & President, Deep Change Inc.

To all, grateful thanks.

TESTIMONIALS

I really enjoyed this book, reading it end-to-end and reflecting on the various tools and exercises that it contains. Peter has combined the philosophy of living a fulfilling professional life with many practical examples, stories and tools that help us navigate and reframe our own beliefs and stories about ourselves. As I embark on my own third career, the book helped me recognise what my true calling is and how that would shape my work ahead.

– **SUDHAKAR RAM**, Group CEO and Managing Director at Mastek Ltd

Making a difference is our greatest calling. Peter's book provides an inspiring route to help you identify your calling and establish your legacy – while building on all you've achieved so far.

– **Dr CAROLYN J. LUKENSMEYER**, Founder & President, America*Speaks*/Global Voices; Executive Director, National Institute for Civil Discourse, Arizona, USA

Why do some doors close and others open? Inspiration from story writing takes you, in Peter Hyson's book, step-by-step into identifying your best self and then finding your true calling, so you build on your successes and leave a lasting legacy.

– **PRABHU GUPTARA**, Advisory Board Member, New Global Markets, UK; Distinguished Professor of Global Business, William Carey University, India; formerly Director, Wolfsberg/UBS, Switzerland

Firmly based on the principles and insights of Spiritual Intelligence, this book can help you become both a better leader and make a difference in the world.

– **CINDY WIGGLESWORTH**, Author, SQ21: *The Twenty-One Skills of Spiritual Intelligence*; President, Deep Change, Inc.

This is an excellent book. What I loved about it was the rare alchemy it offers by way of business insights and reflective exercises, along with engaging stories.

– **GAUTAM BUSHAN**, Managing Partner, LearnTalent, Delhi, India

Sometimes (or is it just me?) it is easy to get to that point in life where you appear to have just about everything you need, but still wake up feeling restless and unfulfilled, thinking "Is this it?" This excellent book by Peter Hyson explains how to lead but also how to leave a legacy. By following his clear and simple step-by-step approach, I was able to work out the things that really matter to me. I loved the book and have mapped out the route to my own legacy. To put it another way, I have moved from "Is this it?" to "This is it!"

— **PHIL JESSON**, author *Piranhas in the Bidet — a snappy guide to better partnerships with your customers, your people and yourself!* Managing Partner, Business Pulse

The role of the leader in business and society is now more challenging than ever before. Finally, here is a book that inspires business leaders and entrepreneurs to identify and integrate their skills and values through creating their unique story that focuses their contribution in the world. Short and to the point, this book packs a punch.

— **ROB CROSS**, HR Director, UK & Ireland, SIG plc

I have worked with many business leaders or entrepreneurs who still have decades of success in them and now feel called to build on that success by contributing to a better world. They would find that these practical activities could help them create just that.

— **GLADEANA MCMAHON**, International author; Editorial Board, Coaching at Work; MD Gladeana McMahan Associates; Chair Emeritus, The Association for Coaching

"When Peter speaks, I listen — carefully."

— **ANDREW MORRIS**, formerly CEO, The Academy for Chief Executives; Non-exec Director, Business Design Centre; formerly Chair Brand Events; CEO, National Exhibition Centre; CEO Earls Court & Olympia

Peter Hyson: International Speaker & Business Author

 **Peter Hyson** is the founder and director of The Spirited Leader. A member of the Professional Speaking Association and The Global Speakers Federation, he has been a keynote speaker to business, professional and special interest groups for more than 20 years.

As well as speaking, Peter also works with a small number of individuals helping them develop their leadership and strategy, in particular using story writing to sharpen their impact and innovation. He is a Chair with The Academy for Chief Executives in London and has taught and mentored entrepreneurs and small business leaders to build strong business and leadership foundations.

Peter has a Masters in Organisation Development and Change Management and is a professional member of The Association for Coaching, and The Writers' Guild. He is also an ex professional swimming coach and continues to be involved in sport having been part of the 2012 Olympics and Paralympics in London, the 2014 Commonwealth Games in Glasgow and the 2015 Rugby World Cup in Twickenham.

Peter has written articles for several professional coaching magazines and is also currently writing a novel set in Wimbledon Village and two screenplays. He is a Magistrate and enjoys living in the Cotswolds countryside – and travelling.

He is particularly valued for his wisdom, insight, challenge and support.

What gets us into trouble isn't what we don't know. It's what we know that just ain't so.

— Mark Twain

FOREWORD

Reading this book was a privilege – it's not like the majority of business books I've read. Peter Hyson offers something different in this guide: it's as if I embarked on a discovery course that he's facilitating. You don't read this book, you do it. And it led me to an answer… Many books don't.

The use of story made a powerfully creative tool to find my purpose, legacy and the answer to the Big Question: 'why were you born?' It's a refreshing, highly effective book. You'll profit from investing in a huge roll of paper or even a big wall.

– MATTHEW BAGWELL
Managing Director, Naked Communications Europe

CONTENTS

CHAPTER 1

WHAT'S YOUR STORY?

At certain times in our lives we reach a crossroads where we know that the decisions we make will determine the path we take and the narrative arc of our personal story as we journey forward. This might be the point at which we have just sold a successful business; when we're about to retire from a fulfilling career; when we are about to take on a new job or role; or even at the start of a new relationship. But, what if we stop and evaluate who we truly are and what we really want from life before we make that decision? Where might the path lead us, and what revelations might unfold if we do so?

The decisions we make determine the path we take

This book is designed to help you evaluate what your true path might be – your life's calling – allowing you to make conscious choices towards a more fulfilling, life-enhancing future.

THIS BOOK IS FOR YOU IF...

- The sweet taste of success is beginning to pale but you're nowhere near ready for the scrapheap.

- You've another 20, 30, 40 years to contribute, so now you want to make a real difference in the world.

- You feel driven, called, inspired – but to what?

- You're willing to dedicate the time needed to complete the Activities and to think about the questions this book raises – because it's an investment in your future.

This book gives you the opportunity to step back and appraise your life, with the purpose and intention of developing a clear vision for your next project. Using your hard-won wisdom and experience, the object of this book is to help you make a real difference in the world, enabling you to gain personal stimulation and satisfaction as you construct your legacy.

Step back and appraise your life

This may all sound rather airy-fairy or idealistic, but in my several decades of coaching in sport, business and through volunteering, I've come across scores of Chief Executives, Managing Directors and senior leaders who have been wrestling with the idea that 'there must be more to life than this'. On the outside, their lives seem successful, but on the inside, there is a deeper calling, a desire to be of service and a need to leave the world a better place. These values are perhaps more common than you might think.

From my work and my own experiences, I know that there is a way forward; that it is possible to follow that inner voice that is telling you to search for that 'something other'. In this book I reveal a pathway towards your future, using tried and tested tools to map the way forward. It is a creative, inspiring, sometimes emotional and frustrating journey, but it is one that will reveal your strengths, your innate values and your destiny, based on all the experience you have gained up to this point in your life. Are you ready to take a leap into your future?

CHALLENGE THE MIND – FEED THE SOUL

Although this book is divided into chapters, there is a continuous unfolding thread to discover – and that is your unique story. So the book will have a different meaning and ending for each reader. The chapters are designed to encourage you to think, reflect, talk and discover your pathway. I do encourage you to work through it in sequence because of its internal logic and coherence. That's not to say that each and every section will take the same amount of time – that probably won't be the case as some aspects of the book will resonate with you more than others.

I have deliberately kept the chapters and the book as short as possible, because it's a call to action and a guide – not a voluminous safety-blanket to warmly and comfortably luxuriate in! My purpose is to be a trigger and an encourager – but you need to do the work.

Here are several notes of caution too: it's very easy to read an Activity and think, "Yes, I've done that before," and either skip over it or even go back to your previous attempt at it. **Please resist** for this very good reason: you've never before been in the place you are now, and you've never been the person you are now, and these Activities are specially designed to progress your self-awareness; to take you deeper and peel back the layers of your persona rather like that of an onion, so that you uncover the seed of who you are meant to be and the gift that you have been uniquely given. And that's not as nebulous as it sounds!

A second word of caution: some Activities will seem completely random. They are. That's because in order to break previous patterns and assumptions, you sometimes have to catch your brain unawares. Your brain is constantly scanning all your senses and incredible amounts of data input in order to spot or create patterns and construct 'sense' (i.e. order) for your safety and security. It does this based on past experiences, but what we're aiming to do in this book is consider a future that's different from the past, where previous assumptions and patterns are being challenged, not superimposed.

You've never before been the person you are now

Through various case studies and from composite client feedback, I also present the insights and wisdom of others who have been through these same uncertainties, and who have struggled to find clarity for their next significant stage in life, or who remain uncertain about how to transform their 'calling' into something tangible. I've spoken to and worked with many people who are asking these life-changing questions and searching for a way forward in their lives. And it's happening with increasing regularity as we enter an era where we are likely to have as much time spending our pension as we had earning it.

We are likely to have as much time spending our pension as we had earning it

The Case Studies presented in this book are from people telling their own true stories. There are also two characters whose stories are composites of the many people I've worked with over the years – they are called Jim and Diya, and they serve to illustrate the unfolding story in a clearer way; they are a literary device to help me illustrate particular concepts I'm presenting to you. But like all good stories, not only do they have the ring of authenticity, they also resonate with real life situations. You will see aspects of them in yourself or in someone you are close to.

The main thing as you work through the book is to be as honest with yourself as possible. It's entirely up to you how much of that honesty you share with others. However, I suggest it's a good idea to talk with other people about your unfolding story as articulating your thoughts will often aid your own clarity. But do it with care, for two reasons. Firstly, this is your personal journey and no one else's – however well they know you, no one can possibly know everything about who you are and who you have the potential to become, because you don't even know that yourself yet. And secondly, many people – even those closest to us – find change difficult or threatening or frightening. They can have a vested interest, perhaps unconsciously, in maintaining the status quo, and in keeping things the way they are, even if the present is quite uncomfortable. For them, it is perhaps the case of 'better the fear you know than the fear you don't know', and no matter how well anyone knows you, they still only know a tiny part of the complexity that makes up the composite 'you'.

Articulating your thoughts aids your clarity

What you won't find in this book are neat answers. You'll find plenty of questions, thoughts, examples, suggestions and processes to guide you, but we are all unique individuals and it's vital that we find our own answers. Indeed, for some of us, that is the nub of what we need to do for the next phase: to stop living a life that has been defined for us by others – be that by our parents, by societal norms or our own misguided anxieties.

In what follows, there is an unfolding and sequential script and various spotlights to shine on different parts of the stage that is your life so far, and still to come. By the end, you will have a clear vision of what the next stage in your life may look like for you, and what you'll bring to it from your own unique gifts. This will then define how you will make a difference in the world (however small) and how you'll gain your own sense of satisfaction and fulfilment.

Stop living the life that has been defined for you by others

You have been interested enough to pick up and start reading this book, so something or someone has opened up this awareness in you. Now it's time to do something constructive and satisfying with the opportunities this book will reveal. Welcome to the age of alchemy!

YOUR STORY SO FAR

Shortly I will invite you to embark upon the first Activity of the book, but before that, take a moment to pause.

Who you are at this point in time is a product of many things that have gone before. Your upbringing, your interaction with parents, carers and other family members, your schooling, your hobbies and recreational choices, random events, your employment, your successes and traumas and your own preferences, likes and dislikes. Some of these will be vivid memories and others are likely to have been deeply suppressed. Some will be known to others; some known only to you, and a few elements of who you are will be deeply buried in your psyche and completely unknown even to you. But *all* have contributed to the rich mix that is you today – the special, genuinely unique you, who has a particular gift or calling, even if you don't know it yet.

So who is this unique gift to the world that is 'you'?

Take some time to ponder on your life and reflect on who you are at this moment in time.

ACTIVITY 1.1 – PLOTTING YOUR LIFE STORY
Timeline 1

Like a writer always does, I ask you to begin with a blank sheet of paper. A1 size is great, but try not to go smaller than A2 as you are likely to find that by about Chapter 3 or 4 you're running out of space. And psychologically this is about thinking big, bold and creative, and opening up, rather than limiting or shrinking because you're literally running out of space.

Much of your life so far has trained you to work from your head and ignore your heart

In fact, my tip to you at this stage is to get an old roll of wallpaper and use a big section from that, because you can then have plenty of room for development, and just roll it up and put it away if you need the space in your office.

You may well have done this kind of activity before but trust me, you need to do it again. You have never been in this 'place' before. Remember also that much of your life so far has trained you to work from your head and ignore your heart. What we are doing here is to seek the balance between writing what your head thinks should be written and what your heart believes should be drawn. Recognise that there is more than one 'true' you. People who know 'you' from one context wouldn't necessarily recognise the 'you' from a different context. There are numerous aspects of the composite 'you' to keep in balance:

- Who you are at work

- Who you are in your relationships (socially, family, closest friends, in a community role, etc.)

- Who you are in your own self (created by the formative events in your history; your desires and aspirations; your successes and failures; your values and dreams)

Recognise that there is more than one 'true' you

Across the centre of a large sheet of paper draw a long line. At one end, mark '0' and at the other, '100'. This is your Timeline and it corresponds to significant events in your life. Now take as much time as you need to reflect on what these events may be.

- The first step is simply to mark these significant events on your Timeline at the correct point. Ideally, as users of mind-maps will know, use symbols and pictures rather than just words because they more readily trigger creativity. But words are fine as well.

- On your Timeline at each stage consider especially what job you had at the time, your friends, family, health, appearance, hobbies and what you did for leisure, where you lived, where you holidayed, any major learning curves, your finances, etc.

- It can be useful to use different colours for different events. For example, I used GREEN for work; BLACK for significant birthdays; and BLUE for holidays, etc.

- Now leave your Timeline for 2-3 days before you return to it. Make any changes you want to and then wait a further couple of days and do the same again. This is because you will be reflecting on the process during the course of your day, and further memories will occur to you.

- Ask friends and family to support the process if there are any gaps in your memory, such as holidays or significant family events – but don't ask for their opinions or memories: just the event itself.

WHAT'S BUBBLING-UP?

"Ask me whether what I have done is my life"

These words from William Stafford's poem, Ask Me raise a theme that will recur throughout this book: *Have I fulfilled my life's calling?* As Stafford infers in his poem, and as Mahatma Gandhi once said, "My life is my message". For example, if I had been a wonderful, talented musician but had always felt too frightened or in thrall to others to pursue that as a career, settling instead for some form of safe form-filling clerical work,

I might well look back and wonder whether what I had done had indeed been 'life'. Has what I have done truly reflected what I am as a person?

But the question for many is, how do we find out if what we have done so far is our life's calling? And more importantly, how do we make sure that our life going forward is the life that we most want to live?

Your 'inner voice' is as different to your 'inner critic' as chalk is to cheese, or Facebook to Wikipedia

The key here is to try to tune-in to your inner voice, your intuition. This is where your true self resides. It takes practice to locate this voice because it may have been supressed for years by the voice of reason or just sheer necessity. There is something deep within me that has been the voice of warning or the voice of encouragement throughout my life. It was perhaps closer to the surface when I was young and struggling to identify right from wrong. And certainly for me, as I got older, I managed to still this voice or inner sense, especially when it was telling me things I didn't want to hear, or seemed to be steering me from the path I thought I should take. But, it's a voice or a calling that won't be silenced. Some refer to it as one's conscience; some call it a Higher Power; some call it God; some simply recognise it as being their inner voice.

This voice – the inner voice – is as different to the persistent voice of negativity and doubt – what one might term the 'inner critic' – as chalk is to cheese or Facebook to Wikipedia. This critical voice is sometimes referred to as 'the voice in your ear'; it nags away at you until you do as it says, whilst your inner voice, that deep knowing, is more nebulous and dreamlike and doesn't have the same impact: unless you actively listen to it.

It is important to recognise that your 'inner critic' is not your true self — it is not your unique voice: you have given it precedence because we live in a culture of fear and competition and your inner critic usually advises caution and restraint — although your inner voice can also be reckless and chaotic, depending on your personality type. In his book *The Chimp Paradox*, Dr Steve Peters refers to this as the voice of the 'chimp' who sits on your shoulder and controls your life. Peters recommends that the chimp brings value only if it is kept under control and in its proper place.

For a long time the voice I heard was the chimp and it drowned out everything else in favour of, "You can't…" or "You mustn't…" It emphasised fear of failure to justify not taking risk. When I first began public speaking, there were at least two different inner critical voices jabbering away inside me. One was the voice of my parents, telling me that I was being pretentious and showing off: what they would probably have described as, 'getting ideas above my station'. Another voice was my own lack of confidence; I knew I could actually deliver the talk — after all, I'd been on the stage since my teens — but this voice whispered that nobody would actually be interested in what I had to say because I was nobody special: a Nottingham lad from a working class background, not an international guru or famous personality.

Each of us has a unique role to play in the world, and doing so establishes our legacy

My response was to listen to my inner critic, so I studied as many popular speakers as I could so that I could copy their style. It didn't work. Of course it didn't; I'm not them and therefore didn't express my own natural style. But it took me a long time and a lot of arguing with myself before I really accepted that it's my story that gives me my authority. And that's all I need, because most people are interested in the stories of other people's lives, and in particular how they've overcome their hurdles. That is what makes us unique and what creates the unique contribution each of us brings to those around us.

Your inner voice is the voice of your true self, dedicated to the task of enabling you to flourish and find your gift or your unique voice:.the thing that only you, because of your inimitable combinations of experiences, gifts, talents and desires can express. Each of us has a unique role to play in the world, and doing so establishes our legacy, our calling.

YOUR CALLING OR LEGACY

What then does that word 'legacy' mean? The Concise Oxford Dictionary simply defines it as, 'a sum of money or article given in a will; a material or immaterial thing handed down by a predecessor.' In effect, it is that which we leave behind us when we're dead. But that is not what I mean by 'legacy' because I am talking about something that is very much alive and dynamic. Your calling – that which insists upon being acted upon – creates your legacy, which comprises of the 'values' you live your life by: very much whilst you are still alive and kicking.

In common parlance nowadays 'legacy' very much carries a positive implication of the values that inform our lives and which leave a lasting, beneficial impact on the lives of other people, or indeed, the planet. For a few, that will be at an international level. For some it will be at a national level. For most of us it will be at a local level, on just a handful of other people: those who are most significant to us, such as our immediate family, our friends and acquaintances, and our fellow workers. This is our direct legacy. But there is also the indirect legacy on those whose lives are touched by the ripple effect of our actions. Recently a CEO told me how conscious he is that his business helps pay the mortgages of his workers' families – he doesn't think in terms of paying a salary but helping support a family. That is a very motivational perspective, which is rooted in his legacy.

Some years ago, I was leading a programme for experienced Deputy Headteachers to help them explore the possibility of becoming Heads. Like many teachers, they were tired, over-worked, stressed and disillusioned. For most of them, Headship was simply additional work and hassle only partly compensated by additional salary. I decided to try something: I got them to close their eyes and imagine themselves back to their first day as a teacher, walking into their new school. Then I simply asked them, "What were you hoping to achieve? What was your dream for your pupils? What did you want for them?" Then after a few moments I simply said, "Headship gives you the chance to do that." Then we moved on and I thought no more about it.

A few years later, I got a letter from one of those delegates who told me that his dream had indeed been to transform the lives of his pupils and he is now running one of the largest secondary schools in Asia – and that calling was initiated by listening to his inner voice, at the meeting long ago. That teacher has impacted literally thousands of lives as part of his legacy. And it is a part of my legacy to make a difference because there must be many more ripples of which I, and each of us, remain completely unaware. Our legacy is intimately connected to our unique inner voice.

It's important to find and listen to your inner voice because it speaks of your *significant* successes and triumphs. These are the ones that show you at your true best, when you are using the skills and gifts that align with your values in the most powerful combination. And because this is your true self, it also speaks of your mistakes and failings, so that you can learn and profit from them rather than continue to be bound or constrained by the fear of repeating them.

The inner voice is one pointer to something 'bubbling-up' but not the only pointer. Pictures or memories can also be significant. Human psychology works on the basis that those things we need to be aware of, to consider and/or deal with, will be brought to our attention. They will bubble up. However we may have established a pattern of ignoring them on the dubious premise of insufficient time or fear that to do so would be just too unpleasant or painful. But, like a volcano, they will continue to bubble away and, like a volcano, sooner or later they will erupt, unless we make the conscious choice to listen deeply to what is bubbling.

So, one of the many opportunities you have in this time of change is to examine those things that are bubbling up for you. It may be a difficult work event or relationship; an ignored bereavement that was never grieved; a missed opportunity still resented; or something you know you need to do but have been putting off tackling. It may be that you are simply feeling ill at ease or discontented without actually knowing why.

ACTIVITY 1.2 – THE BREATH OF LIFE
Timeline 2

So, at this point I invite you to put aside a few minutes, firstly to pay attention to what's bubbling up for you, and then to consider any new insights you've gained.

+ If you are used to practicing 'mindfulness', this is good preparation for this activity. (If not and you would like to try it, I use a digital service called headspace.com that provides guided meditations, but there are others that you can find online.) The aim is not to empty your mind as such, but to focus on your breathing. Just breathe deeply in and hold; and breathe out and hold… Focus on that in-breath and out-breath.

+ After a few minutes, consider the words or events or people that come to mind and add them to your Timeline. The results may seem a bit random or disconnected, but note them nonetheless.

+ Then consider specifically these two questions, adding your response, whatever it is, to your Timeline:

1 What, if any, significant memories came to mind?

2 When were the times when you have felt particular fulfilment or satisfaction? Mark them on your Timeline. What do they have in common?

Very often our most creative thoughts come when we least expect them. But they rarely come on demand. So if something related to this activity bubbles-up over the next few days, mark it on your Timeline. If you can't see anything in common, or any connections between various events of significance, don't worry. All will become clear as you work through this book.

The next Activity focuses on something completely different.

ACTIVITY 1.3 – FLEXING

• Find a way to incorporate five different types of physical exercise into your life. If you have a good local leisure centre, it may be easy to sign up for a weekly swimming session, a gym session, a badminton game, plus a long walk and a cycle. Obviously, choose those activities that you enjoy most and that you're motivated to do.

• Apart from the obvious long-term physical advantages, factoring regular activity into your routine while you're working through this book will release those chemicals that stimulate creativity and energy, which will be essential to your unfolding story.

• Choosing five different types of exercise, will develop different muscles, coping strategies and co-ordination skills, all of which will be useful as you journey on your path.

• Try to keep up your fitness regime, but don't beat yourself up if you miss an occasional session.

SUMMARY

This book is for you if you have enjoyed success and fulfilment in your career – no matter what your age – but cannot imagine doing more of the same for the next 20, 30 or 40 years. This book is for you if you feel called, drawn, or driven towards something, but don't know quite what it is or how to crystalise it.

In this chapter you have:

- Drawn the first version of your Timeline, which illustrates your life story so far, including the different elements that make you who you are.

- Considered the impact of your tastes, health, hobbies, and career and the fact that you are now in a new space.

- Started to scan what is 'bubbling-up' for you; what is being expressed by your unique voice.

- Begun to determine what it is that provides fulfilment and satisfaction when you are consistent with who you are called to be.

NB: Please see page 159 for an example of a Timeline.

"Stories are the secret reservoir of our values; change the stories individuals and nations live by and tell themselves, and you change the individuals and nations..."

Ben Okri

CHAPTER 2

STORIES

WHY DO WE TELL STORIES?

At the end of Chapter 1 I pointed out the importance of finding your own voice, the inner part of you that is the essence of your being. Your inner voice will help to guide you as you build the story of your life, make sense of your past and start to ink-in the details on the sketch of a future that plays to your greatest strengths. Your inner voice flags-up those parts of your history that are important going forward – either to celebrate your successes, or to learn from your mistakes. It helps you to find ultimate satisfaction and enables you to exercise the unique gift you were born with. And it does that by drafting stories in our consciousness.

The place of stories is so significant that stories form the backbone of our lives (and indeed of this book), around which we hang the flesh of our experiences and emotions. We tell stories to ourselves in order to integrate our values, aspirations and feelings and to give the things that happen to us coherence, so that we have confidence facing the future.

For example, when I was eleven years old my class teacher held termly music tests where he called each child to the front of the class to sing a tune that he accompanied on the piano. After I had performed, in a loud voice in front of my classmates, this teacher said, "Hyson, you have a voice like a frog!" From the ensuing gales of laughter and teasing emerged the story I told others and myself for decades: I have absolutely no musical ability whatsoever. For my protection and for my own confidence I avoided any occasion that might have allowed even the possibility of similar ridicule. It took me a further thirty years to discover that I can sing, and that I can follow a melody with other singers. The story has been rewritten because I now know I have some ability. But karaoke or solo singing? Absolutely not!

We also share our stories with other people. We do this because we want their validation and approval that our stories make some sense of who we are. The anecdote above served as an ice-breaker at parties and as an excuse not to participate in certain activities; but in the end, in the re-telling of the story, it has allowed me to enjoy singing and has opened new doors for me.

Key turning points and their significance in life often only become clear in the later telling of them

We also tell stories because the very act of articulating them and sharing them with others, aids our own clarity and understanding of who we are. It is our attempt to reconstruct the past, relate it to the present and then interpret it to give us confidence and coherence as we face an uncertain future. Key turning points and their significance in life often only become clear in the later telling of them; they are often much harder to spot in the moment of living them.

This is fine for when we are seeking coherence, but one of the foremost emotions of the 'wilderness' – that place where the past no longer satisfies but the future is at best indistinct – is chaos not cohesion. When you are in the wilderness the defining feature is that all the stories you once told; all the things you once tried that worked so well and brought success, no longer work – or have any real meaning or satisfaction.

You may be wondering what on earth is the point of even bothering to look back, never mind searching for trends and links if the whole point is to move towards the future from a past that no longer satisfies? And to a degree, you're right. The defining feature of what you're currently experiencing is indeed that the old assumptions and ways of doing things no longer hold true for you, and furthermore, they cannot provide you with the satisfaction and sense of achievement and contribution you seek in the next phase of your life. One of the key elements of this book is to look forward in an imaginative way, allowing fresh insights into your life and making room for a paradigm shift of values, rather than more of the same.

But, that does not mean you leave behind the previous decades of skills, experiences and knowledge that you have accrued. That would mean that your life up to this point had no purpose. No, what I am suggesting you leave behind are the old patterns and ways of linking them that were limiting you in some respect.

MAKING DIFFERENT CONNECTIONS

The key to this new phase of your life is not to change or deny the past but to make different connections between the key points in your life – to see them in a new light. The ability to see connections afresh and then apply them in a new context is the beginning of the greatest distinguishing feature in the next stage of your journey: wisdom.

Leave behind the old patterns that were limiting you in some respect

There is nothing wrong with the way you have previously made connections: they may well have been entirely appropriate for those stages you were passing through; now they have simply served their purpose and need to be either discarded or re-engineered and upgraded to serve a different purpose and to tell a different story.

Some things will, of course, be better left behind, like my decades-held belief that I totally lack any musical ability. Similarly, there was a particular project that I once led that I had always viewed as an abject failure because of the way it ended and I had both shunned that area of work and avoided the people involved; but recently I met someone who had been part of that team and she told me how important it had been to her own professional development and success. When I saw it through her eyes I developed a completely different interpretation of the project, and I could see that the type of help she'd valued from me was a theme I could spot across other projects as well. So, what needs to be left behind there is my limiting perspective of the situation, not the situation itself. When I made these new connections, thanks to my colleague's retelling of the story, it became a significant event in my life.

Making different connections becomes inevitable when your motivation and focus changes – when your sense of purpose moves. It is entirely natural to us. Often in the first years of our working life, for example, we focus on gaining those skills and experiences that make us stand out and prepare us for promotion, for rising in importance and power in the pack. We can even be quite selfish in our determination. Or we focus on those skills that will give us the competitive advantage in negotiations or spotting the next business opportunity. But then, over time, as our motivations change and our perspective becomes wider, we perhaps become more aware of the needs of others, the longer-term effects of our work, or the future prospects for our children. So we make new connections and create new stories to fulfil our aspirational motivations.

Similarly the focus of this book is for people who have become aware that there is something else that they're called to do; who have a new sense of giving back and of wanting to make a difference. In order to define what that calling is, changing our patterns of thinking and making connections that are different to the norm, can open up doors that may previously have been shut to us.

Just as your physical body changes and develops over the years so does your thinking and emotional development. You are both the same person you were at fifteen and someone completely different. Looking back at your life and seeing where you might have limited your your potential allows for the possibility of change – it is never too late to realise the potential of those experiences, if you have the courage to make new connections and retell your story.

ACTIVITY 2.1 – TELLING TALES

+ Look back over your Timeline and pinpoint a significant event in your life, that you feel was either traumatic, or a failure.

+ Retell that story to create a different conclusion. You can be playful here and make people do things they didn't, or make things happen that allows a different resolution to evolve. Enjoy the process, be imaginative, and make different connections to the ones that actually happened.

+ What difference might this new story have made to your life?

+ Do you recognise any limiting behavioural patterns or inner critic voices that curtailed or impacted the original event?

The purpose of this activity is to show that making different connections can really open up the potential of any given situation. Doing so in a fictional way is safe and enjoyable but also helps us to recognise previously limiting patterns so that we are less likely to repeat them in future.

What about those times when we just *cannot* see links and connections? Do they serve any purpose or value? Is there a lesson to learn?

When we fail to make continuous links between what has gone before and what is happening now, the story we tell about ourselves feels as if it is unravelling. And it is. Without a coherent story, we feel inauthentic and at a loss. It is particularly important to look carefully at these occasions where we feel our story is unravelling, because if they are 'blind alleys', the question is, what motivated us to go down them? What did we want but not get, and why? It is important to consider where doors closed, metaphorically speaking, in order to avoid any side-tracking in the future.

REVISITING YOUR STORY

At various points in this book, I'll invite you to revisit and reframe your story, to draft and redraft it – just like every author does – as bits are added or discarded and as the next phase, your legacy, becomes clearer. Ultimately, I anticipate that you will reframe a story that's exciting and motivational to you, and that draws you towards your legacy.

Stories are incredibly useful and important in envisioning your future and clarifying your focus, because they can go beyond the current boundaries in which you find yourself; they can be exploratory, challenging and transformational. But for them to be *relevant* to your true self and your calling, an important question emerges for the first but not the last time: what exactly do you want for the future and to leave as your legacy?

It is worth pondering on this question. Somewhere on your Timeline you could start to make a list, or draw some symbols that link to your future aspirations. This may be an aeroplane as a symbol of your desire to travel, or a book symbolising your dream of writing your memoir, or a pair of boots to symbolise that fundraising walk along the Camino trail. However vague or insignificant these feelings or aspirations for your legacy may be, note them down now, and see if they transform or hold true as you work through this book.

What exactly do you want for the future and to leave as your legacy?

If you're in business, one of the things you learn early on is the importance of telling stories. In fact, most businesses are founded on a story or a dream. I know of a company that was set up to manufacture windows because the owner needed some for the house he was building for his family. "I couldn't find any windows on the market that I liked, so I decided to set up a small manufacturing unit in my wife's stables, much to her chagrin, and make my own. Ten years later, I sold the business to my son and retired with a lucrative nest-egg," he told me.

It's not just business people whose stories define who they are and their motivations. I cannot think of any great leader who was not also a consummate storyteller, and all the more so when they used the power of symbols in their storytelling. Martin Luther King had a dream, and he told the story of that dream in a memorable speech, the ripples from which still reverberate more than 50 years later. Interestingly, Nelson Mandela chose to tell the story of his long walk to freedom and his transformative values of reconciliation and forgiveness by wearing a South Africa rugby shirt – long since the symbol of white supremacy – to present the post-apartheid Rugby World Cup to South Africa's winning captain. Words could not have said more.

More prosaically, from the sales executive embedding the key features of their product into their sales pitch, through to the manager touting for a promotion, or the Board executive presenting to shareholders or potential investors – the most potent weapon in their armoury is their skilfully crafted and expertly told story. When I have been involved in interviewing hundreds of potential volunteers for major world sporting events, the outstandingly successful ones do not just regurgitate a list of things they have done, they become alive and glow with the stories they remember of someone they spoke to or helped out, or learnt from. Facts may convince the head but stories convince the heart and are more potent in prompting decision-making.

Facts may convince the head but stories convince the heart

A well-told story can inspire, motivate and turn around a particular situation or event, with lasting impact. The best leaders learn from the past – both immediate and distant – and use it to sculpt a new future that they communicate with vision, passion and commitment, via a story. The stories are clear, honest, realistic and inspiring. You owe it to yourself to do the same with your life story, because, as they say, you're worth it.

Stories also operate at the physiological level: they help to steer the line between calculated and uncalculated risks. This is vitally important since uncalculated risks release cortisol that induces the fight/flight/freeze response, whereas calculated risks release adrenalin and endorphins that accelerate learning and positivity.

Leaders may often hear one story but need to re-draft it into a different context: maybe an additional significant detail is unearthed that they can use to illustrate their own point; maybe the audience is different; maybe someone else's comments trigger an 'Aha!' moment and a new insight; maybe the author simply wants to look at something through different eyes and therefore takes the same incident but explores how each character might view that same incident differently? Hollywood directors and scriptwriters call this iterative process a 'rewrite' and a story may go through five, ten, fifteen or more rewrites before arriving at a satisfying, compelling version. Your own story is likely to go through a number of rewrites too, as you delve further into this book.

As any storyteller or indeed stand-up comedian will tell you, the best stories are iterative: they come alive when they are re-told; this is the alchemy of interaction between the teller and the listener. Many a writer will recount that they suddenly got a new insight or understanding of their work in this way, even after many deliveries. So, at different points over the next few chapters, I will invite you to redraft your story or some parts of it, to see what new insights might emerge. There is such richness and variety in our lives that it takes many sittings and much reflection to begin to see the essence emerging. Five years ago things might have been different. Five years on they may be different again.

Stories have been part of our very nature ever since our ancestors sat in the cave by the fire and told them as a means of passing on truths, skills and values; as a way of passing time and learning how to appease the gods. They gained their colour and life through constant telling and retelling. Details got added or left out. Emphases changed. The essence remained fundamentally fixed; the surrounding details and especially their interpretation or meaning or significance were fluid and highly creative.

However, the likelihood is that you have been trained to write in a way that is anything but creative. You are likely to have been trained to write in order to pass examinations or submit dissertations or get business reports accepted. And in the drive to avoid the red ink of the examiner or boss, you will have learnt to write in a style that is properly structured, grammatically correct, solid and with a complete absence of energy or magnetism; the result is what writing coach Tim Morrison calls 'beige'. After nearly half a century, I can still hear my schoolteachers admonishing me to, "Just stick to the facts!" And while that might be appropriate when I sit on the bench as a Magistrate, it's the kiss of death when I sit at my desk as an author. And even less helpful when I seek to discern my future.

That need to appease others or quieten their voice of criticism by acquiescing to their demands often continues into later life, so that ultimately, you cannot hear your own voice because it is drowned out by the voices of others telling you what you need to do, or ought to do. These voices are usually overlaid with a heavy accent of self-interest.

SOWING THE SEEDS OF LIFE

One of the things an author does is sow the seeds of future developments as the story unfolds. It seems to me that our own life contains similar seeds, not all of which have yet to sprout above the ground. Indeed, some of them may have lain undisturbed and subsumed for many years. When severe forest fires decimate large swathes of countryside, the following spring heralds a flowering of species that have for decades been unable to force their way up through the dense undergrowth, but thanks to the clearing of the fire, can now enjoy their time to blossom in the sun. This is a lovely metaphor for the seeds in your life that are yet to flourish – and flourish they will, sometimes at what seems like the most unlikely of times, perhaps when it feels like a metaphorical forest fire has swept through your life and destroyed what you held most dear. This book will help you to locate and cultivate those emerging plants through to fruition.

In the desert of transition, your story will be the oasis that sustains you

These 'seeds of life' come in all shapes and sizes; an acquaintance of mine worked for years for Greenpeace until she had a life-threatening illness. This brought her to a time of reflection where she realised that her passion was plants, and so she set up her own nursery specialising in useful, edible and wild species; the seeds in her life were the moments when she went on team-building events in the great outdoors where she realised that the reconnection with nature fed her on a spiritual level.

So, if you are at this point of major reconsideration in your life, because someone or something has applied the flame-thrower and burned away much of what previously grew there, I have designed the following chapters to give you the opportunity to find some green shoots of new growth – allowing the blossoming of that which you might not yet be able to imagine.

So let me invite you to take stock of where you are; a compass bearing in the present in order to prepare for setting your future course; the one that will carve out the direction of your journey, and craft your legacy. In this, your unfolding story will be especially important. Your story is what reminds you of your meaning and purpose so that in the desert of transition, with its sense of uncertainty, insecurity, fear and loss, your story will be both the oasis that sustains you and the filter in discerning what lies ahead. It will give you on-going meaning, satisfaction and legacy. It will also help you learn what you can afford to leave behind, what you must leave behind, and what, at all costs, you must keep hold of in the future.

ACTIVITY 2.2 – LOCATING YOUR RESERVOIR OF VALUES
Timeline 3

The first steps of your Timeline dealt with the facts, but picking up on what Ben Okri remarked at the beginning of this chapter – *Stories are the secret reservoir of our values* – I invite you to take things a step further.

- Go back to the events marked on your Timeline and consider what feelings, skills and values flow out from those events.

- Where do you see your values most clearly displayed and when are they most under threat or compromised?

- Look at each event: not just the jobs but also your hobbies, volunteering, evening classes, bereavements, even holidays. You might also find it useful to look at other things you have written over the years: letters, journals, diaries, speeches, reflections etc.

- Then ask yourself the following questions, giving yourself the time and opportunity to reflect and jot notes on each one before moving on to the next. This is your future life you're investing in. It is worth the time it takes!

1 Identify those times where you feel you invested your time wisely. And also pleasurably.

2 Identify things that give you energy and joy.

3 What are energy-sappers? (These might be events or people.)

4 Mark the highs and lows, the unexpected, the times of uncertainty etc.

5 When were you using your greatest strengths? With friends? Family? At work? At leisure? As a neighbour? As a volunteer? Mark these times on your Timeline.

6 Are there any times when, according to your own assessment or from other people, you were particularly courageous? Note them.

7 Where are the turning points (often more obvious with hindsight than at the time of experiencing them)? These are the events where, for one reason or another, under your control or not, your life took off in a new direction. Mark these as 'Key Events' in a different, identifiable colour.

8 Now take as long as necessary to look again at your Timeline. Can you see any patterns arising? Mark these using a symbol that you identify as a pattern (such as a dotted line). What does this tell you about your feelings, skills and values?

9 Finally, looking back with the wonderful benefit of hindsight, what themes are unfinished? These may be unfinished for a reason, for example, because they were doomed to fail, or because you didn't enjoy them – but if they were unfinished because other people sewed the seeds of doubt in your mind, that is worth noting, because it may form an underlying pattern.

ACTIVITY 2.3 – LIFE'S LESSONS
Timeline 4

Leave some time between this activity and the previous one to allow your thoughts to deepen and expand. Then, go back to your upgraded Timeline once more, which is now enriched with your feelings, skills and values. This time you are searching for the lesson you have learned from certain significant events in your life.

◆ Go to each of your 'Key Events' and draw a straight line out from each of them. Write on each line, 'Lesson Learned' and then write one or more things at the end of the line that you feel you value or draw upon from this experience (much like you would on a mind-map).

Take some time for reflection. If you can do it right now that's great: if not, schedule, commit to and protect the time when you will reflect on this process and findings.

If you're familiar with mindfulness or meditation these techniques will certainly be a good preparation for the work you are being asked to do here. I certainly recommend that you silence the telephone and any other potential distractions. If it helps, have a notebook to hand but only use an electronic one if you won't be tempted to crosscheck your emails!

CLOSED DOORS

Have you ever been in a situation when it felt like the doors of opportunity were slammed in your face? For example, you'd sent in what you thought was a fantastic application for a job and you didn't even get an interview, or you offered to help at a local youth club and were told that your support wasn't necessary? It can be hurtful at the time, but these are significant events in your life, because like it or not, they propel you in another direction.

Quite often when doors are closed to us, the situation is labeled with words like 'regret' or 'rejection' or 'if only': if only we'd been allowed that opportunity, so much would have been different (i.e. better). If only that person hadn't turned me down... If only they hadn't offered that promotion to someone else... That label becomes the story attached to that event, heavily steeped in disappointment and remorse. Sometimes, the door is closed as a result of our own decision that we may later come to regret (although not always). It can feel like a door closed if you had to choose between two options: marrying the 'wrong' person; choosing the 'wrong' career; backing the 'wrong' person at work...

If it isn't immediately obvious what your life was trying to tell you at the time of a particular door closing on you, go back to that event and consider it as if you are an author looking at the plotline of a story. What different direction could the story have gone in if the door hadn't closed? Try one or two ideas. There will probably be one that really strikes you. If not, maybe there just is no particular lesson to be learned.

ACTIVITY 2.4 – WHEN ONE DOOR SHUTS...
Timeline 5

Now let us take the work you have done so far, a stage further.

+ Look at your Timeline again and try to discern the times where doors have closed at a certain point in your life. It may be your choice: for example, you resigned from a job or left a voluntary role because you no longer felt comfortable there. It may have been forced on you: perhaps you were dismissed from your job or you failed to get a promotion. It may be a decision that you made at the time: not to start a relationship or not to go travelling, for example.

- Looking back now, if your life was trying to tell you something at those points, what was it? When doors close it is often because you need a prod in a particular direction. What was the direction you were propelled into? Did it make you happy?

- Many films and novels use this device to send the hero forward even though they may fail to realise it at the time. Can you identify moments in your life where one door shut and another one opened?

ENERGY GENERATORS AND ENERGY SAPPERS

Now we turn our attention to events that stand out because of the effect they have in terms of energy levels, not just physical energy but more importantly psychological energy. One of the greatest energy-sappers, at least for most people, is bereavement. Others may include divorce, redundancy, house relocation or a major health scare. Long periods of stress or extended periods of excessively long working hours similarly sap energy, as does multi-tasking.

Some events have the exact opposite effect. For example, for some people divorce can come as a relief rather than devastation; redundancy reduces some people to lethargic inertia and for others can release almost frenetic energy.

Energy generators are those people or events that literally do top-up our energy levels. For me they vary from 20 minutes on the rowing machine that also boosts my creativity levels, to time spent with great friends, to watching a really good comedy programme or spending time in mindfulness.

These energy generators and sappers have further significance because they relate to our core values. At the simplest level, energy-generators indicate that a core value is being met and energy sappers flag up where a core value is being denied.

In an ideal world, there would be no energy-sappers. They serve no useful purpose. But in the real world they cannot be avoided entirely. The habitually negative co-worker is a fact of life; total avoidance is never going to happen. But that does not mean you have to spend more time in their presence than absolutely necessary; nor does it mean you need to keep negative friends within your circle. But as a rule of thumb, where you have energy sappers, either people or events, it is vital to build in sufficient energy-generating people and events to ensure your energy levels are topped up.

ACTIVITY 2.5 – TOPPING UP THE ENERGY TANK

I would now like you to take a large sheet of paper and divide it into three columns.

- The first column is headed **Key Events & People**
- The second column is headed **Energy Generator or Energy Sapper**
- The third column is headed **Therefore I Need To...**

Look at your Timeline and select some Key Events: these go in Column 1. Then assess them for Column 2. For example, if I work with people who present as being continually negative, critical and undermining, my energy is sapped quicker than air escaping from a punctured balloon so in Column 1 I would name a particular person I worked with at a key point in my career who was always complaining and putting the worst possible explanation on every decision. In Column 2 she would go down as an Energy Sapper. And in Column 3 I would make a note of what I needed to do to minimise her impact on me (for example avoiding her at lunchtime or after work or by making sure I increased the number of positive conversations I had).

One of the key activities that generates energy for me is writing because creativity and innovation feed my soul. In Column 3 therefore, I might regularly refer to writing as an energy-generator. So: Column 1 – holiday in Crete; Column 2 – energy generator; Column 3 – wrote the preliminary notes for my novel.

KEY QUESTION: Do you notice any trends emerging that you need to take into account in planning your future direction? For me, I had five times more references to 'Writing' as any other energy-generator, which indicated that this may be part of my legacy. These trends might be things you absolutely must build in or things you absolutely must avoid. Note these down in this exercise.

MEET JIM AND DIYA

Jim and Diya are composite characters from the many people I've worked with over the years, who have been asking similar questions to those we deal with in this book, and who have wrestled to find satisfying answers. Nothing happens to Jim or Diya that has not happened to the people I have worked with and coached in real life; neither do they do or say anything I have not encountered in others. They'll flag up key learning along the way and act as illustrations of key points. The first is 'Jim Preston'.

The door of Jim Preston's top-of-the-range Jaguar closes with an almost imperceptible click. A distant purr indicates the engine has been turned on and a muted swish accompanies the wheels as they begin the journey of transferring Jim from office cauldron to domestic tranquillity. The discrete digits of the dashboard clock remind Jim it is 19:05, that the evening is young; and he has had a successful day. A very successful day. He's also aware that this will soon be reflected in his bank account: a bank account that mirrors the burgeoning waistline of his mid-50s body. Every inch the successful Managing Director.

He glances across at his briefcase (leather, high-end branding as befits his status), smiling with pride at the bulging contents that contain his copy of the just-signed contracts: another prestigious client on board. He pictures the office as he returned in triumph, waving the signed documents above his head like the returning conqueror, to the appropriate accolades from his staff.

As he pulls out of the car park he notes with pride the lights still burning in his offices: it may be seven in the evening here, but that simply means half a world away, business is just beginning and already his enthusiastic team is preparing to hunt for the next client to be sucked up in the corporate fishing nets. He can see, feel, smell their enthusiasm, their hunger for success. We'll soon need some new offices, he thinks. Now, where do I fancy this time?

But no sooner has he envisioned this than he has to pull over to the side of the road. He is shaking. He feels nauseous. His normal fifteen-minute drive home tonight takes almost an hour. And as if he did not feel bad enough already, the shock he sees on his wife's face when he walks in through the door is almost worse. Luckily, actions speak louder than words and before he realises it, he is sitting by the fireside with a glass of wine and a bowl of olives and crackers.

"I'm absolutely fine. Probably just a virus doing the rounds. Everyone at work has had something." Except he knows he is not 'fine'. Far from it. That nagging feeling is back like indigestion.

If Jim thinks his facile brushing-off of his wife's enquiries is the end of the matter he vastly underestimates her. She simply gives it a couple of days to settle down and then when no disease manifests itself she picks her moment over an evening meal. "Come on, Jim. What is it? I know you too well."

"It's nothing. Everything's going really well. We've just won that big contract with Garretts; there's two or three more in the pipeline and we're well ahead of our sales targets. It's all great." Deep down he knows that's not true; and deep down he knows it's wishful thinking that Sue will let it ride. And before long, he has to admit that even he does not actually know what is gnawing away at him. "Just give it time. It'll settle. I promise."

But soon it's not just Sue. Others at work begin to notice. For a while he knows he can drown-out their doubts. After all he's been running the business for nearly thirty years so he is adept at not necessarily showing his hand too soon, and he's familiar with the dark arts of distraction and misdirection. Not for the first time, Jim is grateful for the hours spent playing poker.

The trouble is, he can't fool himself. Time, then, for a new project, he thinks. "Okay, team, we're looking for..." What? For the first time in his career he has no idea.

Over the course of the next three days his team bring suggestions: a rival firm that has just lost its main client and is ripe for take-over; an exciting new material has been developed by scientists that's just been presented at an obscure symposium which has lots of promise... but each idea fails to excite him. After perhaps a dozen suggestions are uncharacteristically shot down in flames his team leave the conference room, closing the door heavily, bordering on a slam.

A few days later his Chairman is even more robust: "Get your act together Jim, or you'll get your cards." He hates the pitying looks in their eyes: if only it were that simple.

He tries, but with his heart no longer in it he is increasingly bypassed by his colleagues. And one look into his wife's eyes and he knows he is on borrowed time before she demands a further 'we-need-to-talk' talk. This can't go on.

Knowing that is one thing. Knowing what to do about it when you have absolutely no idea what the "it" even means, is quite another. All he knows is he is tired and is not in the least sure he has the energy or the appetite, to start another cycle of intense business investing and growing.

Which is why at 2 am on a Friday night/Saturday morning Sue finds him in their back bedroom office surrounded by a ramshackle pile of books, journals and papers. On his laptop a smartly dressed trim-figured male stands frozen mid-stage, a large illuminated TED sign behind him and overhead a banner proclaiming 'How to find your Path'. Before she can say anything a loud snore momentarily frightens the life out of her before she realises its source. She frowns and retreats once more to the empty bed.

By the time Jim emerges, bleary eyed and unshaven at eleven o'clock the following morning, Sue has had enough. "Jim – I have just one thing to say to you. What do you want? Because until you can fathom that out, nothing is going to change. And if it doesn't, well, you work it out... And by the way it's your turn to take Matt to swimming training. Here."

Jim ducks and just manages to catch the large sports bag before it strikes his head, then, grabbing a folder from his office and a son from the computer, deposits everything into the family car en route to the pool.

An hour later and Jim is on a sparsely cushioned and sparsely populated bench high above the local swimming pool, scribbling away on a notepad. There are some things that can still only be done with pencil and paper he reflects, embracing procrastination. Somehow, the physical act of gripping the pencil, the free flow of graphite across the blank white space, prompts reflection in a way he's never been able to do electronically, however sophisticated the word-processing and mind-mapping. Maybe it's a generational thing, he wonders.

The noise in the swimming pool is unbelievable, echoing and reverberating from the tiles and roof. But Jim has been doing this chauffeuring for almost three years and has developed his own mental soundproofing every bit as good as ear plugs. The piece of paper on his lap is already a spiders' web of lines and words and symbols and he is so immersed in it that he has no idea someone has sat next to him until a woman's voice and accompanying nudge in the ribs penetrates even his insularity. "Not on speaking terms today then, Jim?"

He smiles at Matt's best friend's mother, and narrowly fails to discard his handiwork before her inquisitive gaze. "Hmm, writing your life story are we then?"

"Actually – yes. Though not in the way you mean. I'm just making a note of some of the things that have happened to me... Anyway, it doesn't matter. I needed a distraction."

"Oh come on. You know me better than that."

"No. Really. I'd rather..."

She stares at him for a few moments. "So, let me guess. Something's going on at the moment. You don't know what it is. And Sue's getting pretty fed up with it? Right?

"How...? Has she been...?"

"Of course not. But I do see you here every other week and it's not exactly difficult to spot. So – have you had the ultimatum yet...? Ah, I guess you have!"

Jim grabs his papers and struggles to his feet, his face a mix of horror, anger and disbelief.

"Jim, it's okay. You forget: Chris and I do this for a living. We see this all the time in business."

"Doesn't give you the right to..."

"No it doesn't. You're right. It's just that you looked so... out of sorts. And we are friends. Anyway, up to you. But if you think Chris could help... Okay, subject change coming up... How's the little man's training? He's looking good."

Some conversations just refuse to go away, no matter how much you might want them to. And some things are too important to let go, like a marriage and a career. Which is why a week later he is sitting in Chris' faux lounge-style consulting room shuffling several pieces of paper and still wondering what on earth he is doing sitting here with a Business Coach, whatever one of those is. Chris has already been at pains to point out he is not a therapist or a counsellor – but it doesn't stop Jim feeling he is sitting in a surgery of some sort: paranoia being something of a hobby for Jim.

Now forty-five minutes in, even Jim would reluctantly agree it is not going too badly. If you like that sort of thing. And Chris is actually quite easy to talk to and surprisingly, well, wise.

Jim's papers are spread around his lap and around his feet. They have been coalesced into a rough chronological sequence, which in itself has helped him feel more at ease: there is, after all, some order. Chris waves an arm over them, revealing an interesting pair of cufflinks that Jim resolves to ask him about later. "Jim, looking over all of these bits of paper ('that's my life' thinks Jim, 'not just some random bits of paper'), which events or stories are the most important to you? Apart from Sue and the kids, who you've already talked about."

"Well, I think that was when I first joined this engineering company, Brighams, and turned it around…"

"Anywhere other than work?"

"I'm not sure… Yes, I guess way back in my early twenties when I took over coaching an under-15s rugby team. That was a fantastic time."

"Okay, so when did that end?"

"Well, I guess when Brigham's needed more of my time and I also met Sue at about the same time – that's when that door closed."

" 'Closed doors'. Tell me more about that."

"Well, that's what it felt like. There were a whole lot of things that I might have done: getting a coaching ticket; maybe moving up the ranks but the door to it was closed because I needed the time for other things. In fact, when I look at these sheets there have been several closed doors. Those are the ones where there are no lines drawn out from them: they just seemed to peter-out. Or sometimes get slammed shut."

"Okay, Jim, over the next week or so I want you to look particularly at the ones that you describe as 'slammed shut'. What do they have in common? And what was the impact? Did they leave you feeling disappointed and drained? Or energised and excited? And then how are they connected?"

The second character who is living through these very same stages is Diya Mandal.

Diya Mandal pauses outside the Boardroom door, draws out a wodge of papers, takes a deep breath and flings open the door. Her heels click as she walks to the head of the deeply polished table. Each member rises and applauds. She nods to several as she passes then reaches her chair and sits. The others follow suit. For a moment, the only sound is the jangling of the bracelets on her wrist. Then she stands. "Gentlemen…" (and it is only men), "Montgomery Digital is sold for the sum of £43.4 million!" She inspects the faces of a dozen people round the room: pleasure, pride, excitement and maybe a hint of greed. Yet all she feels is apprehension. Of what, for goodness sake? Her role is secure – at least for the next eighteen months: that had been a condition of purchase. And this is hardly the first time; in fact it's her third sale, so she might even call herself a dab hand by now. So where is the energy, the drive, the hunger for the next meaty project?

Moments later, those thoughts have passed. The Board's enthusiasm is contagious and she hears the welcome popping of a champagne cork. Not that she drinks alcohol; but it's enough of a success symbol to lift her spirits. "Gentlemen – a toast to Montgomery Digital – past, present and future!"

Before she has even left the room there is an email request for an interview from a business journalist. She sighs but replies to suggest she contact her PA and set something up.

The setting-up turns out to be only a couple of hours later, as Diya sinks into the leather upholstery at her favourite Members' Club. She notes with some relief that they are still in the late afternoon lull that follows the lunchtime rush and late afternoon busyness, and so they are neither overlooked nor overheard. A tray of tea and biscuits is served for them. The journalist seems nervous and perches uncomfortably on the edge of her seat so that Diya expects at any moment to see her slip off into a crumpled heap at her feet.

"Now, about your father's textile business…"

Diya stiffens: why does everything always start with that? Yes, he is one of the biggest importers of Indian cotton; yes, he's one of the biggest employers in that part of Lancashire; but isn't she doing just as well in her own way? Do they think even her success is down to him…?

"Ms Mandal?"

"Sorry. What were you saying?"

"Ms Mandal, I asked if you had ever thought about joining your father's business?"

Thought about it? It was all her father ever thought about. It is always the first thing he says to her when they met up, which consequently is no longer frequently. And her siblings too. But that is the stuff of family drama not newspaper columns, especially business columns.

"No. My father has always recognised that I need to establish myself away from the family, in my own right. So let me tell you a little about…"

"But didn't you think it would be easier if you'd... or did he help you set up, um..." She looks frantically at her notes.

"...Montgomery Digital? No, he most certainly did not." Diya's tempted to point out that the journalist wouldn't have dreamt of asking that question of a man. "Everything I've done – and this is my third company don't forget – everything I've done has been on my own two feet."

"Oh, I didn't mean to... Sorry, I..."

"Look, let's get this straight. My father has an outstanding business brain and so do I. We simply choose to use them in different ways. He has his areas of expertise and I have mine. We are different. And we each respect that." Diya isn't quite sure just who she's trying to convince. "I've never taken a penny from him for business and I never will." And he'd never offer it, she thinks. "Now, I thought this interview was about successful women entrepreneurs? So why don't I tell you a bit about the three businesses I've built and sold while you gather the questions you want to ask me. I started off in my cousin's textile business (nothing to do with my father's) when I was fourteen, just generally tidying up and moving the bales of materials back and forth. But customers kept asking me questions and I soon realised I was actually pretty good at selling. So I persuaded Aarush to train me. And by the time I was eighteen I knew as much as he did. And because I had an eye for colour and for what would sell, I became his buyer, then the manager. I even started importing the material. By the time I was 25 I got a loan and bought him out. And by the time I was thirty I sold it for £1.5 million."

The journalist vainly tries to keep up with the invective while still searching for her list of questions as papers spill out of her rucksack. Diya could almost feel sorry for her.

"How does that sit with your father and your family traditions?"

"How...? Look, let's get this straight. For my generation we make our own decisions. Times have changed and women expect to be treated exactly the same as our male counterparts: we expect to be judged on what we can do. And that has nothing to do with my father or my country of origin or even my sex – that's just who I am! Now why don't you try me with some of the questions you'd ask any other successful entrepreneur and let's see where that gets us."

"Right. Ms Mandal... When you sold that first business, what made you go into electronics rather than carry on in textiles?"

"Now that is a good question. Fundamentally, I wanted a new challenge, something that would give me new energy. And probably, if I'm honest, something that would prove to my family that I could be successful in other areas as well. Probably even prove it to myself. So when I heard that Leeds Electricals was looking for an investor I jumped at the chance. Turns out I could transfer my skills because seven years later I sold my share for £5.5m."

"Ms Mandal, I hesitate to ask this but you are a woman and didn't come from any sort of electrical background, so did you...?"

"Did I find it difficult to be taken seriously? Yes, I did at first. Especially when we started getting really successful. Jealousy, I suppose. But the results soon won my Board and shareholders over. And it just became more and more difficult to ignore me. Mind you, ignoring me never has been easy. Especially because turning that business around really got me energised. I just loved it."

"So why did you sell?"

"Oh, that's easy. Once it reached a certain point it just needed managing and that's not me. I got bored with it. It needed someone with different skills. It was a pretty easy decision, really. And by then I'd spotted a gap in the market so I simply set up a company to exploit it."

"Which was another new area for you – digital? Surely that was a bit risky?"

'My investors didn't seem to think so. I had a really strong business case and yes, a couple turned me down. But when I met Montgomery Finance they got it immediately and made it clear they would be in it for the long haul. They spent time really trying to understand what I was about, why I was doing it, and what drives me. I learned a lot from that."

They're interrupted by a persistent tapping on the door. Diya frowns: her staff know far better than to interrupt her when she's in a meeting. Her secretary slightly opens the door and pokes her head around.

"Miss Mandal, I'm so sorry but it's your brother on the phone. He says it's urgent and he sounds upset. Shall I...?"

"Put him through."

The journalist rises to tactfully leave but Diya waves her back down as she lifts the telephone receiver. Then she goes pale, grabs the edge of the seat and gasps..
"What happened?"

SUMMARY

In this chapter you have:

+ Learned how to use your Timeline to identify the Key Events in your life.

+ Identified your values and their impact on those key turning points and closed doors.

+ Identified what saps your energy and what generates energy in your life.

CHAPTER 3
FINDING COHERENT THEMES

When an author starts writing a new story, one of the first stages they go through is research. This is just as true for most novelists as it is for the non-fiction writers. Effective research adds a sense of authenticity to what they write. Speaking to people who have experienced the story's themes will not only give huge insights into motives and values, but will also yield anecdotes that resonate with a ring of truth. The writer will then skilfully weave these into a coherent and satisfying core narrative held together by three or four coherent themes: the warp and the weft of the story. Unlike weaving however, there will be loose ends, as there are in real life, but for the reader there is a sense of an unfolding direction; there are a few clues scattered in early chapters that hint where the narrative might be going. There will be sudden changes of direction, unexpected events and a series of hurdles of increasing intensity that must be overcome before the hero faces a crucial trial where the outcome genuinely hangs in the balance.

The storyteller will construct a web of events that help the hero progressively realise why the past has irretrievably passed (Act 1) and why they are now thrown into the wilderness where they must explore countless unknown perils and obstacles (Act 2) before that final battle on the borders of the new beginning: will the hero defeat the monster, meet the girl/boy, win the sporting medal, catch the killer…? This narrative arc is called The Heroic Cycle, where the protagonist comes full circle through these trials and knows herself for the first time.

You may feel your life doesn't have the inherent drama of a Hollywood-style film, but believe me, all the epic themes are there in your life nonetheless. So, over the ensuing chapters of this book I will draw on the skills of storytelling to help you pull together the scenes of your life to date and then build on them for the final Act – the dénouement. And like all good stories, not only can the early scenes and unfolding components be pulled together in several rather contradictory combinations, so the story will develop and grow even as you tell and retell it, before it is fully formed.

From the moment you start telling the story of your life, you will have begun to discover some moments of revelation, some of surprise, some that you even thought you had forgotten and maybe wished you had forgotten! They will emerge and take on form and flesh as you tell and retell your story. And even then, the story will never really be quite complete.

What will emerge with growing clarity are recurrent themes and I will help you identify these and weave them in different ways until you feel you have created a satisfying, inspiring and purposeful story of the past as you currently understand it, and as a vision of the future that will prove satisfying and rich. I call this 'alchemy', because it is indeed weaving the threads of the normal into the gold of legacy. This is not being pretentious: this is identifying your unique gift and contribution to the world. These recurring and coherent themes from the past provide significant signposts for the ensuing acts of your story, both of things to build in and of things to avoid.

We are weaving the threads of the 'normal' into the gold of 'legacy'

Before looking at this further I invite you to once again revisit your Timeline and your Story.

ACTIVITY 3.1 – THE WARP AND THE WEFT
Timeline 6

In this activity we are looking for some coherent themes in your life: links and connections that show a pattern of thinking or action that may be limiting in some way, or indeed may be the catalyst for change and growth. Take some time to focus on these questions and note them on your Timeline, either with symbols, connecting lines or key words.

+ What are the things that have driven you to make the choices you have made at key moments in the past?

+ What part was played by others' expectations? By a psychological wound e.g. death of a parent, parents' divorce or your own?

+ What assumptions continue to underpin your current life script?

+ What might prevent you venturing to reinterpret the past in order to re-vision the future with the richness of its potential?

+ Where do you notice consistent themes emerging?

FACING UP TO UNCERTAINTY

Uncertainty is an inherent part of life itself and the lifeblood of a novel too; but it can be a thoroughly unpleasant part of life, especially if you have no idea where it is leading or what the future holds. The more you have at least an inkling of direction, a vision of where you are going and a sense of purpose, the less uncertainty has the power to sap your energy.

Part of the reason you are in a time of change is that the world itself is in a phase of unprecedented uncertainty and change, which is happening at a more consistently rapid pace than at any other time in human history.

In most parts of the world, people are living longer: the average life expectancy in the US and the UK is almost 80 years, while in India since 1960 it has increased by more than 50% to above 65 years. My parents' expectation was to retire at 65 and enjoy perhaps 5-10 years beyond that. As a Baby Boomer I can reasonably expect to continue to be healthy well into my 70s; Millennials can have a reasonable expectation of nearing 100 years of age. Salim Ismail, former innovation director at Yahoo and Founder Chair of Singularity University reckons, "We're adding three months to life per calendar year". With it has come an increased expectancy from life.

Historically, the greatest expectation from life was simply survival. Leisure was an almost unknown concept. Industrialisation revolutionised both how and where we worked; then mass communication enabled businesses to function across the world; and also allowed entrepreneurs to flourish in their own homes. Not only has the concept of leisure emerged, but in itself, it has become an industry. The net result is that people not only expect to have work but also to have leisure time too – and for both to continue over a longer period of time. Therefore our impact on the world, both positive and negative, is greater and more significant than ever before.

Since for most people the general trend is towards increasing affluence and choice, so our demands increase. We expect our cars to be more sophisticated as well as more efficient; we expect our television to cover more channels and at our demand; we probably have more clothes in our wardrobe at this moment than our parents owned in their entire lifetime! More tellingly however, we expect a sense of fulfillment, of meaning, from life. Where our ancestors expected merely to survive, we expect to thrive.

With greater choice and power also comes greater responsibility. We will have more impact on the world than any previous generation. It is our choice whether that will be constructive or destructive. That will be our communal legacy. The fact that you are reading this book and working on its Activities suggest not only are you also aware of this but that you also want to make a positive difference and leave a lasting legacy. The downside of increasingly complex choice, however, is the increased difficulty in 'seeing the wood for the trees' – of discerning how and where we feel called to make that difference. We are, literally, spoilt for choice.

This change in life expectancy inevitably affects the demographic at work, not just in terms of age but also of our assumptions of what we can expect from our career. For example, according to the British newspaper The Daily Telegraph, in May 2010 the average age of 3,302 Directors on Boards of FTSE 350 companies was 58; for CEOs it was 53; and for Chairs, 64. Further research as late as 2014 does not significantly alter that although it does reveal that Gen Y and Millennials (those entering the workforce since 2000) are now reaching senior executive level in their 20s. According to a Daily Telegraph survey of people heading-up British SMEs (businesses employing up to 400 people and a turnover of around £3m per annum), about 10% are aged 35 and under and a further 25% are under 45. A similar number (33%) are aged over 55 (May 2010).

These statistics are telling, because not only are people achieving career goals at a much earlier age, but they can expect to continue in paid employment for another half-century or more. What kind of role will a CEO be looking for after 20 or so years at the top of their game? The answer is, one that allows them to develop their legacy.

Of huge significance is the change in expectation of those in the workforce. For example, the authors of the report *Leadership Traits – Insights for Today, Pathway for the Future*, argue that the emerging Millennials/Gen Y (who constitute up to 23% of the workforce in 2015) are more ethically aware, more appreciative of differing viewpoints and expect to see a social dimension to work. They are typically more cognisant of the wider world and issues such as poverty, hunger, climate change, war, natural disasters, famine, etc. They are also determined to enjoy their work, which must align with their values, and will resign if these values are not met. They have little concept of a job for life (after all, they have hardly grown up with experience of it) and the previous progression of education-work-retirement is meaningless to them. Rather than viewing work as progressive and sequential, they expect it to operate in phases with the ability to take several 'gap years' for travel and then return to work but also to spread learning and skill-generation across their working lives. And many recognise that in order to have the standard of living they desire, they will have to work later into life to achieve this.

Those entering the workforce since 2000 are now reaching senior executive level in their 20s

This means that the workplace will be unrecognisable in the coming decades to what it is now. It will need to be flexible, dynamic, ethical and future-proof to live up to the expectations of Millennials. This could be a very good thing, both for people and planet, but it will certainly shake-up the values of the Baby Boomers and later generations.

While that is happening at one end of the work spectrum, there is considerable change at the other end too. For, with increased longevity, expectations from life have changed. For large parts of the world, increased leisure and increased spending power broaden choices and prompt questions that would never have occurred to previous generations, especially what is it exactly that people want and expect from life? Even 'retirement' has become a flexible, almost meaningless concept with increased opportunities for short-term paid projects, consultancy and even full-time employment well beyond 65. And woe betide the retirement home or village that fails to offer high-speed broadband! The depths of expectations of later-life care and provision have yet to be fathomed.

Whilst you may be familiar with Abraham Maslow's *Hierarchy of Needs*, what may be less well known is that in later years, Maslow added a further developmental stage beyond self-actualisation: he called it self-transcendence or 'the spiritual'. He found that the healthiest, most developed adults were not the 'self-actualisers' he identified earlier in his career, but the 'self-transcenders': those who moved beyond ego into service to others and the whole of society. (See Appendix.)

level 5	**self-actualisation** creativity, autonomy, learning, personal growth
level 4	**esteem needs (ego)** approval, status, prestige, self worth, self-confidence
level 3	**love needs (social)** to be loved, cared for, friendship, relationships sense of family, tribe, class, territory
level 2	**safety needs (security)** shelter, protection from harm and from disease
level 1	**physical needs** food, water, warmth, immediate escape from danger and pain

He concludes that self-actualisers are self-focused where as self-transcenders literally transcend that and are more concerned with their impact and contribution to the wider world. They define their purpose in terms of work being meaningful, helpful, promoting justice, about spiritual (not religious) fulfillment and the highest possibilities of human potential. Maslow also argues that they are more likely to be innovators than the self-actualisers because they have a clearer sense of the 'ideal', the 'potential' and the 'ought-to-be'. They are more likely to view themselves as temporary custodians of talent or skill or leadership – and more committed therefore to passing this on to others. They are significantly more likely to be interested in a "cause beyond their own skin". (Maslow, 1969). Many speak of a sense of 'calling' – and he found them across all life sectors.

You are likely to be a self-transcender because of the questions you're currently asking and the future contribution you're looking to make. The quest on which you are engaged would be one that is familiar to transcenders, and they serve as a reminder that there is hope of fulfillment. The process of change has already begun.

ALL CHANGE...

People may react to change in several ways: some simply deny it and try to carry on as if absolutely nothing has happened, despite all the evidence to the contrary. They build a neat little cocoon around themselves and have to work increasingly hard to maintain it. Others will change the absolute minimum necessary and cling on to as much of the past as they possibly can. A third group will accept it but insist that it is a temporary state before everything goes back to 'normal': the way it was before. Another group will actively embrace change, snatching it almost the moment it appears. And there is an infinite variety of in-betweeners.

Humans have a remarkable ability to adapt to the most unpleasant of circumstances, finding just a crumb of affinity sufficient to enable survival. This is sometimes referred to as the Comfort Zone: the place that enables us to function in the face of oppression or injustice; even when we are being undermined or subjugated, because we can identify just enough positives to make it bearable. The Comfort Zone can help tolerate the bullying boss because it may ultimately lead to the next promotion; it will help justify excessive working hours for the same reason, or because we need the money. But, and this is important, the Comfort Zone will also serve as an excuse to avoid change. Its one common feature is that medium- to long-term, staying in your Comfort Zone can *never* provide satisfaction or fulfilment. It means you can identify just enough positives or at least neutral elements to enable you to survive but you will never thrive in this environment.

However, often the only alternative to the compromises of the Comfort Zone can seem like entering the wilderness or the desert of uncertainty – which may be where you feel you are at the moment. To escape the Comfort Zone change is absolutely necessary; but with change comes uncertainty, chaos and bewilderment. If this is how you are currently feeling, don't despair! At least you've left the confines of the Comfort Zone and this book will lead you through the wilderness to new horizons.

SOME COMMON QUESTIONS

Am I going mad? Whatever has prompted you to look at the world – or at least your future part in it – with new eyes, it can seem a very strange place to be. No wonder many of the mystics of past ages took themselves off into the desert to contemplate the meaning of their life.

The desert is an interesting analogy. It is an uncomfortable and disorientating place to be. It is a place of extremes, typically roasting hot during the day and desperately cold at night. There is a constant threat to our safety when we are in a desert. It is a place where a sudden sandstorm can wipe out our tracks and redraw the terrain in a matter of minutes.

But it is also a place of great beauty and tranquillity and where an oasis can refresh both body and spirit. A desert is a spiritual magnet attracting countless wise men and women who have felt called there for contemplation and insight, and more recently visitors are attracted there for the silence and the clarity of the sky and stars.

And, a desert is a much safer place to be with a little foresight: some planning and some basic equipment such as food and water, a compass and some protection. And preferably a guide!

The desert is a great metaphor for the place we can find ourselves in when in transition from one phase of our lives to the next: it can be a scary, isolating, disorientating place; or it can be serene, meditative and ultimately transcendental – depending on our state of mind. When we enter the desert, we can expect to return transformed in some way, and this is exactly the case for the spiritual desert we can find ourselves in at times.

You are not going mad – you are experiencing transformation

We ask the question of ourselves: 'Am I going mad?' when we're experiencing new and scary thoughts, emotions and energies. Because we don't recognise them and feel threatened by their unfamiliarity, we wonder if it's all an illusion we're creating: that we're going mad. But very often, we're just in the wilderness of the desert. We need to take the time to ascertain what lessons the desert is teaching us about our resilience, our ability to embrace change and be comfortable with uncertainty. We are not going mad, we are experiencing transformation.

One of the themes in this book is that life is constantly throwing-up clues to help understand who you are and where you are at your best. In that sense, the old cliché of life as a journey is important because it is preparing you for what is to come. You cannot contribute your legacy without the travelling to get there. CP Cavafy's poem Ithaka puts it beautifully:

"As you set out for Ithaka
  hope the journey is a long one,
  full of adventure, full of discovery..."

And I concur with this: a journey that is full of adventure and discovery is a treasure indeed, because it provides so many clues along the way that guide you towards your true calling.

Am I the only one facing this? Clearly not or my book would have a severely limited market! However, we have only just begun to feel we can ask these kinds of soul-searching questions. This is partly a generational thing: we have had a longer period of sustained growth and development than any other generation in history, despite recessions. The vast majority of previous generations had to spend all their working life providing for basic survival and anything else was irrelevant, especially esoteric questions about the meaning of life.

"Money doesn't make you happy; it just allows you to be miserable in greater comfort."

From the middle of the last century in the Western world and perhaps a generation later in other parts of the world, a growing number of people gained the financial security to begin questioning what else they wanted from life. It was a difficult question to share with others, especially those of the generation that had experienced world conflicts and massive economic and social uncertainties. It sounded ungrateful to have gained a degree of economic freedom and then to be asking what to do with it because it did not prove as satisfying as had been promised. The materialist goodies dangled under our noses as enticing motivators, provided only transitory satisfaction. As one pundit remarked: "Money doesn't make you happy; it just allows you to be miserable in greater comfort."

However, alongside this has come a greater emphasis on medical and psychological research into wellbeing. It has become acceptable to talk about feelings and there is a much greater understanding about human needs above Level 3 of Maslow's Hierarchy (Level 1 being 'basic survival'; Level 2 being 'safety and security'; and Level 3 being 'social belonging'). Therefore, the higher levels of 'self-esteem', 'self-actualisation' and more latterly 'self-transcendence' have become significant as aspirations. The rise in the use of business coaches has validated this area outside clinical counselling.

Is this simply a mid-life crisis? Yes, in part it is, although it can happen at any age. But it's not the conventional Western sense of a vain final attempt to regain a long-lost idealised youth – it is a life crisis in the sense that it is characterised by a growing realisation that most of what you have spent years yearning and fighting for can actually feel very empty and unsatisfying once you have achieved it. It may fill your bank account but it fails to fill your heart or your soul. For you though, this is about rekindling that sense of purpose or calling and giving something back: its about altruism and legacy – perhaps even changing the world.

Is this about changing careers? Not necessarily. It's about finding out what really makes you come alive; it's about finding the essence of you. Sometimes, but not always, that's connected with what you do for a living, but often it can be about looking beyond the constraints of work life to the creativity of self-actualisation.

Find out what really makes you come alive

But how do you know you won't simply be jumping out of the frying pan into the fire? You don't! The hard reality of this stage is that there are no more guarantees of success than there have been in any of the previous stages of your life. But I can guarantee that if you stick with more of the same you will remain there – in the frying pan. Remaining in your Comfort Zone may numb the pain for a few months like a painkiller, but it will not cure the dis-ease.

The good news is that you are now better equipped through your hard-earned experience and your emerging wisdom to spot some potential pitfalls earlier, and therefore avoid them rather than fall into them. One of the features of this stage of your life is a dissatisfaction with the things that have got you thus far; or at least the drive is to reapply them in new directions. Although you retain those skills, the context in which you find yourself is fundamentally different.

The transition between self-actualisation and self-transcendence is exactly what Jim Preston is facing, and his story continues below.

JIM'S STORY

A few months later and Jim reckons that far from getting better, his situation's actually getting worse. Even his friends have now begun to notice how distracted he can be. So as he sits down for supper one night with his wife, he decides it's time to broach the subject once more.

"Sue, this stuff with Chris is all very well but it's not solving anything. Okay, I can see that I'm not doing the things I thought I would when

I was in my teens, but then who is? It's all very well thinking at that age that you'll change the world, but real life isn't like that."

"Isn't it? Why not?"

"Because you get a mortgage, a wife, children, staff, other commitments..."

"Oh, so we're to blame, are we?"

"No, that's not what I'm saying. I just mean other things, important things, take over. Priorities change. I changed."

"Really? Are you fundamentally a different person?"

"Yes. No... Fundamentally I'm not that different. I guess my... values... are still the same. And now I suppose you're going to ask me what they are, those values? Oh God, I'm even starting to sound like Chris, aren't I?"

Sue smiles and waits.

"Okay. I guess honesty. Excellence. Getting results. Helping others do their best. Being creative; being able to find better ways of doing something... But it just feels as if there's still something I'm missing..."

"How about you put all your notes up on the office wall and we'll have a look at them together over the weekend? And maybe someone at the supper party will have a bright idea?"

That Saturday night Sue and Jim are relaxing around their dining room table with four friends. Candlelight flickers across the ceiling and the third bottle of red wine is breathing. As the plates empty of the main course and people are noticeably relaxed, there's no sign of Jim broaching anything more challenging than the current 'Scandi-noire' television series. Sue has had enough.

"Question for you guys. Jim is looking for a new challenge. What would you suggest?"

"Join the Golf Club! I've never understood why you haven't done it already. All that fresh air and exercise. Plenty of time in the bar..."

"No – buy a boat and sail round the Med. You've always said you wanted to travel. Here's your perfect opportunity. We hired one and did it for a month last summer: I'd do it again like a shot. And you still get the fresh air and exercise of golf – just under blue skies rather than rain."

"Yeah right!" Sue isn't impressed. "You can just see me in a bikini like some dolly-bird on the deck? I'd be a laughing stock. Maybe we could just travel – train sounds good."

"What about space travel? For a cool quarter-million…"

Which is about as helpful as it gets. As their suggestions get ever more extreme, Jim isn't sure whether to be relieved he's off the hook or frustrated by a lack of insightful suggestions. He was hoping for a bit more from his friends.

Why is it so difficult, he muses? None of these are exactly unappealing ideas, but none are compelling, either. They're almost like… treading water. And why should I just turn my back on all my experience? It was tough enough getting it. I want to leave something behind after all that hard work. And I'd really feel a loser if I wasn't playing the game as hard as everyone else, but… I just can't imagine enjoying that place again.

His Coach recommends networking. An internet trawl shows a conference the following week: Mining Gold from the Second Half of Life. He registers with a feeling of resignation, and he wasn't to be disappointed. "Oh God, Sue, it was full of bright-faced men – and it was all men – telling me how much my life could bring me joy by volunteering with remote jungle tribes or some needy folk in inner cities. I ask you! Me? Surely there's a company that can make use of my skills, not just my time and money?"

He even tries a few speculative job applications: a new government think-tank for encouraging engineering apprenticeships; a consultancy placing interim senior managers – but none feel right. None leave him feeling he'll make much of a difference.

Weeks later and he's swinging between despair and frustration. Nothing gets better or clearer, in fact it gets worse. He's already cancelled two sessions with Chris; but, since he's also a friend, he feels compelled not to cancel another. Yet more navel-gazing, he mutters as he rings the doorbell.

If Chris feels any reaction to being stood up he's too professional to show it. But he does cut straight to the chase: "Jim, last time I asked you to look back at those doors you described as being 'slammed shut'. What do they have in common?"

Jim consults his notes, where the connecting lines have multiplied like some tapeworm disease. "Actually, there are two groups. For one of them I closed the door, because I just knew it wasn't the right thing for me. The others were slammed in my face – they were out of my control. But actually, now I come to look at them again, I've just noticed something interesting. They're actually all linked: just before the doors closed, almost without exception, I was feeling disappointed and frustrated. It's as if I was sensing I was being sucked down a route that was draining me, stopping me from being at my best. Because when I look at my peak times they're a long way away from the closed doors."

"So let's look at your current role. You said last time you were really energised and excited when you got it. Why was that?"

"It offered so much potential. I could turn the business around, we could really expand our products and there were some great people there, and I could make the most of their potential."

"When did that change?"

"I guess when I started to get bogged down in meetings, when I kept getting told I was the only one who could do it, the one the clients wanted to see."

"What did that prevent you from doing?"

"Finding new markets, new products. Being creative, strategic. And actually just being around, so the staff could drop in when they needed to."

Finally Chris challenges him: "Would you recommend your career to your children?"

"Absolutely not – no!"

"Right, then. I've got two questions for you for next time. What were you passionate about as a teenager? And what inspired you then? Go and think; and don't leave it so long next time!"

ACTIVITY 3.2 – MAKING CONNECTIONS

Consider these questions and write down in your notepad the
first things that come to mind as you ponder them. Repeat the
question several times as you write to nudge your sub-conscious.

1   Am I living a whole life now – or a deferred life?

2   What makes me come alive? (Note the first thought, even if
    it's facetious – there will be an element of truth in it.)

3   What would feed my soul at this point in my life and going
    forward?

FINDING THE PATHWAY

It is possible that you may have reached a similar point to that
so graphically portrayed by the writer TS Eliot in his poem
The Journey of The Magi. The wise men return home from their
visit to the new-born baby Jesus "… no longer at ease here, in
the old dispensation, with an alien people". One event, one
encounter and everything familiar has changed and can never
be the same again.

Their journey was something they knew they had to do,
something they felt drawn towards. But they had no idea what
the impact would be on them. I suspect that even on the way
home they still had no idea. It was only when they tried to
settle back down into their old life, the 'old dispensation', that
the emptiness of it became apparent. Nothing else had changed.
Only them. So everything had changed.

It may be that what has brought you to this point is nowhere
near as dramatic as this, even if there is an identifiable trigger
event. It may be the sale of a business; it may be the moving out
of the final child from the family home; it may be a bereavement
or an inheritance or even a lottery win. Or it may be that you

have no such identifiable trigger event, simply that now you have finally acknowledged something that has been gnawing and growing for some time and has, at last, reared its head above the surface and you can ignore it no longer.

So what is the way forward? It is all very well identifying and analysing what has brought you to this point. Finding the way forward that will satisfy the new challenge is perhaps proving surprisingly difficult to find. After all, you have built up huge knowledge and skill; you know how to run a business or organisation with outstanding success and you have access to all sorts of people and information. Yet there is no single key to unlock the successive doors to your future, even if you know where those doors might be located.

BUT follow the steps in this book and all will become much clearer.

> "Knowledge is knowing a tomato is a fruit; wisdom is knowing not to put it in a fruit salad."

I have failed to find the source of that quote but it is a neat descriptor of the two main phases of life and the precipice between them upon which you now stand. This is the period that writers call the 'inciting incident' that closes Act 1; it marks the hero's challenge to leave behind previous assumptions and step out into the unknown wilderness of Act 2. It is a period of gaining knowledge and then applying wisdom. The story of your life unfolds in a new direction.

THE ELEMENTS OF A CLASSIC STORY

All stories have a basic structure, which may vary in shape and size, but which holds the story together. Without it the reader is likely to feel lost or disorientated, disappointed or let down and even irritated. At the same time, the reader couldn't necessarily pinpoint or name the structure. It's just always been an inherent part of the stories we have been told, heard, read or invented from the days of cot and kindergarten onwards. That same structure is present in films, stage plays, television dramas and soaps: it may just be a beginning, middle and ending, or it may be significantly more complex and multi-layered, but it gives the story a boundary and a pathway. It takes an author of uncommon skill to break these conventions without leaving the reader dissatisfied.

Joseph Campbell wrote a classic tome on this: *The Hero with a Thousand Faces*. His book follows the archetypal 'hero' who, as the story unfolds, ventures forth from the familiar world into one of supernatural danger, there to encounter numerous monsters and opposing forces before winning the decisive victory and returning to wealth, love and acclaim. Key stages on the journey involve a call to adventure; a road of trials any one of which might prove fatal; and then a supreme battle and triumph that results in the great gift that the hero returns to share. Three Acts, though not of equal length. Applying these to examining our past and projecting forward prompts some interesting and at times uncomfortable insights.

In most stories there is a constant sense of change and also conflict (internal and/or external), tension and discontinuity. Which is exactly what you may be feeling at this stage in your career. The world has changed, the old has irretrievably passed away and the new future, the new beginning, is not yet clear. Welcome to Act 2! It is the longest, most complex and, often, the most difficult and challenging.

ACTIVITY 3.3 – CAPTURING YOUR STORY

Write your life story so far using the elements of the classic story I have explained above: you are the **protagonist**, the main character, and I want you to identify those events and/ or people who have acted as **catalysts** for significant changes in your life. As part of the plot development, weave in your significant **trials, tribulations, defeats and victories**, and then identify the **turning point** that has brought you to this present place or the moment you realised you were called to make a difference in some way. Note that at this point, I am not asking you to write the ending. That is yet to be unveiled, but I am asking you to write your life story to this point where you are now.

Crucially, remember that a good story does not consist of a long list of cold facts; its heartbeat is the emotions that are flying around. Pay particular attention to how you were feeling at particular times; when you were excited; when you might have been afraid; when you felt insecure; when you were 'flying' with success; when you felt proud; when ashamed.

Draft and redraft your story. Tell and keep 'retelling' it, both to yourself and to those around you. Once you have the basic outline, the plot, try telling parts of it in the genre or style of your favourite authors: e.g. history, romance, science, action thriller, comedy. How does that change your insights?

I appreciate this is quite an undertaking; it can take years to write one's memoir – but this is not what I'm asking of you. I'm asking you to filter out the key factors, people, events and feelings that have been pivotal for you. Don't worry about it being good, or readable: it's your story, however you want to tell it and it's not going to be published (unless you want to, of course), but it is an opportunity to be playful, provocative and creative.

By the way, don't get unduly concerned with the factual accuracy of your stories. At best our memories are incomplete and frequently embellished and reinterpreted. Start with the known facts: for example, I know I was born on a particular street on Hyson Green in Nottingham, UK and I can visualise the physical house. My memory will draw out some pictures of events that happened there and will then helpfully create details to fill in the blanks! As you create your own stories look for significance in the details your imagination fills in. These can be at least as important as the 'facts' you recall. Many of the stories we tell of our past would probably not stand up to rigorous scrutiny if a time machine allowed us to revisit them; elements of imaginative embellishment will have occurred and this is fine, because this flows out from the very human need to make sense, to create meaning and connections; without that we're left feeling dissatisfied and our brain hates a black hole. If it can't find an explanation or a meaning, our brain will simply create one, whether fact or fiction, so that the story can be compartmentalised and dealt with.

There is always significance in what you remember, what you leave out and the actual words you choose. You were a different person at different times. People who know 'you' from one context would not necessarily recognise that 'you' in a different context. Recognise that there is more than one 'version' of you although there are some very important core elements and these will form the building blocks for your next Act and the satisfying knitting together of these various threads.

Which is exactly what Diya is finding…

DIYA'S STORY

For some reason, when you learn about the death of a parent, you never forget the place you are in when you hear the news. It's imprinted in the memory forever. For Diya there follows an uncertain period of numbness that eventually melts into anger. Before the funeral, her brother Pranav calls her into the family factory – she assumes it's to do with tidying her father's possessions from his office. She had always loved the sense of homely chaos of her father's desk, from which he had been able to locate absolutely anything in under five seconds; something of which he had been inordinately proud. Even when she sees her younger sister Vani she feels no warning. But then she notices they are both sitting across the desk and behind it she's startled to see another figure. Her blood runs cold.

"Uncle Rakesh..." she bows.

"Diya, sit down. This is not the time for me to beat about the bush. You have had your time to be selfish and to have your fun, but now you need to face up to your responsibilities. You are to take your father's place and run this company. You will start next week."

Had she not been mourning her father's death she would not have been as slow recognising what was coming. But it hits her like a bolt of lightning. Shock, then horror: this is what she's dreaded and spent her whole working life getting away from.

Then anger – hot, seething anger. Having fun? As if running those companies had been like a few days at a funfair?

"Uncle Rakesh, let me be absolutely clear. I have spent almost twenty years getting to where I am now. And there is no way on earth I'm going to throw it all away for – this!"

"And let me be perfectly clear, Diya. This is your duty. This is not some whim. Your family needs you to do it and do it you will. The matter is closed."

He rises and walks calmly out of the room leaving the siblings shuffling: two in embarrassment and one in rage.

"Don't even think about it," she storms. "I'd rather..."

"Diya – calm down. We know it will take some getting used to; none of us really saw this happening. He seemed so fit..."

"Pran, are you deaf? I'm not doing it. End of... I'm more than happy for you both to run this business – to have it..."

"Don't be stupid, sis." This time it's Vani, as she jumps to her feet. "How on earth do you think we'd be able to run a company like this? I've still got a year to go at Uni and Pranav? He can't run a bath never mind run a business."

Pranav is about to protest but quickly realises it's probably in his best interests to take the insult.

"That's not my problem. Dad knew all along I had no intention of taking over. If he didn't plan his successor, it's hardly my problem."

"He didn't exactly plan to die, you know."

Diya stands and moves towards the door. "Look, I'm more than happy with what I'm doing. It's just not going to happen." Yet even as she says it she knows it is not true. There's been a gnawing dissatisfaction for some time...

But the conversation won't go away. Several sleep-disrupted days later she is leading a seminar at a national conference. During the breaks in proceedings she chats to old friends and colleagues, but as she broaches the subject of what legacy they'll be leaving, or what the future might hold, it is soon very evident that no one seems to understand her dilemma. All they want to talk about is how they can use the conference to grow their business and especially their contacts. Conversations that previously might have occupied her for twenty minutes drift into silence after three or four minutes, pretty much the time it takes her to explain what she is looking for really.

Am I going mad? she wonders as she tramps back into the hall for the afternoon session. Am I the only one who's feeling dissatisfied with life? But no matter how hard she tries, her concentration has gone; the topics, once core to what she wanted, no longer hold her attention. Under the guise of note-taking she flips open her electronic notepad and starts to search. Now, what would be interesting? Rather flippantly she thinks, 'Dis-ease'! Hmmm, close on half a million entries. Then her eye is caught by a fragment from a quotation: '... no longer at ease here...' Promising. The link makes her jolt back in the chair. Apparently it is part of a poem about the Magi, whoever they are, returning from some visit. But what strikes her is the expanded text:

"... no longer at ease here, in the old dispensation, with an alien people."

That's it. That's exactly what she feels like: an alien in what should be familiar territory. She has been trying to get back to the way things were before her father died, but 'the old dispensation' is no longer comfortable. This really is the wilderness.

She recollects a phrase from someone who had sat next to her in a previous session, almost bouncing up and down in excitement: 'this is what feeds my soul.' She'd not taken it in at the time; she'd considered it a little flaky, possibly because she hadn't warmed to her neighbour. But now it hits her with red-hot intensity. It describes exactly what she's been feeling, what she's been missing, that vague ache of something absent from her life. It could almost be described as a hunger.

Her work is her food; she's often described it as her food and drink: what keeps her going, fresh and challenged. Of course she's feeling hungry! For the first time in years, she doesn't have a project to get her teeth into. Clearly it's withdrawal symptoms from the challenge, the thrill, the pressure of the company turn-around. That's easily solved. She reaches for her laptop and enters into the search engine 'businesses for sale'. Two hours and several hundred entries later she shuts the lid impatiently. Not a single thing of interest. And heaven knows she's tried hard enough, even reading the small print in her desperation to find something, anything of even the remotest interest. Nothing. Except those nagging hunger pangs.

ACTIVITY 3.4 – FOLLOW THE LEADER

+ Name four leaders you particularly admire. They can be living or dead, real or fictional, famous or unknown.

+ List what you admire about each of them individually.

+ Where are the similarities between them? What does that tell you about yourself and your aspirations?

PREPARATION FOR TRANSITION

In this chapter you have spent a lot of time looking back over your life. This is important in identifying themes, trends and characteristics, and to see where you have built skills and experiences, and where you have felt limited or challenged. You have begun to construct the story of who you are.

You are currently in a time of transition: a stage between holding on and letting go; between arriving at the precipice and jumping off. In this time of transition, incremental gains may be more sustainable than an irrevocably big decision. It can certainly be a time for trying out new possibilities.

Now you are employing the 'alchemy of wisdom'

Finally in this chapter there is an active step to take.

ACTIVITY 3.5 – FROM INERTIA TO ACTION

As you look back to the last Activity and the characteristics you have identified, use them to outline the broad areas where your next project *might* occur.

If, for example, you identified 'Innovation', what practical steps can you take over the next four weeks to move towards a goal that allows you to be more innovative? How and where are you at your most innovative? When do you have your most creative ideas? Are there people with whom you need to have a conversation about this?

You are now taking a calculated risk of moving forward from your Comfort Zone. It is adrenalin-releasing and endorphin-charged.

You may have been hovering in a state of uncertainty for some time, so this next step may seem dauntingly unclear. But it is only a step – it is not a leap of faith, or irrevocable in any way. Inertia is fatal to action and without action you will never get to the next stage successfully. Please don't make me quote that over-used phrase about even the longest journey beginning with...[1]

SUMMARY

In this chapter you have:

◆ Uncovered some coherent themes in your life and the impact of considering them in new ways or with fresh connections.

◆ Used the elements of the Classic Story to capture a creative way of reinterpreting your story, enabling you to gain new insights and prepare for the transition from the present to the future.

In effect, you have been employing the alchemy of your wisdom.

"There is a tide in the affairs of men,
Which, taken at the flood, leads on to fortune;
Omitted, all the voyage of their life
Is bound in shallows and in miseries.
On such a full sea we are now afloat;
And we must take the current when it serves,
Or lose our venture."

Julius Caesar, Act 4, Scene 3

---

1 ... the first step!

CHAPTER 4
REFRAMING YOUR STORY

Over the next few chapters, the consistent theme will be to take another look at familiar stories from your past and to do so in new ways. There are several reasons for this. One is that it gives you options, different escape routes if you will, from your Comfort Zone. Reframing your story allows you to see possibilities that are currently hidden. Another reason is that events that have happened to you in the past can be connected in a number of different ways with equal validity, but produce very different outcomes and interpretations to those that actually happened. There may be times when various elements overlap, rather like the moon and the sun during an eclipse: producing the 'tide' which 'when taken at the flood, leads to fortune', as the Bard so aptly puts it. You can probably look back to a handful of times when this 'confluence' has taken place and the outcome has been significant.

For me, it happened when a seven-year work contract ended at exactly the same time as my marriage. I had the opportunity to renew the work contract with more of the same, but that really did not feel the right thing to do. I knew I needed a new challenge but I was unclear what that might be. With hindsight,

I would say I knew I was being called to something without that something being in the least bit clear. I pushed at doors in several different but familiar directions, to no avail. I was offered a couple of things but just knew they were not right for me at that time. As more doors closed behind me, what began to emerge was the most radical of all and came as a result of another set of convergences.

A friend offered me free accommodation for one year; a business acquaintance offered to sponsor a short training course for me to attend; I was offered some interim work – and my consultancy business was born. Not only did the components begin to fall into place, but somehow, it all *felt* right. *Carpe diem:* seize the day.

Those same overlapping opportunities; that same eclipse or tide may never coincide again, and if missed:

'all the voyage of (our) life
Is bound in shallows and in miseries.'

Well, shallows and miseries may be rather extreme for the decisions you currently face, so let's stay with the rest of the quotation and accept that:

'on such a sea we are now afloat;
And we must take the current when it serves,
Or lose the venture.'

It may be worth looking back at your Timeline and using that quotation to see if it applies, either way, at previous intersections in your life. If so, what do you learn from the outcome? Was there something you avoided, perhaps because of fear? Was there an opportunity you were not able to take because, perhaps, young children meant it was not practical to move house, for example? Or maybe the opportunity felt too risky at that time? The point is that at the stage you have now reached, you are being offered the opportunity to review past decisions, learn from them and decide what will and will not be relevant in the next stage of your life.

MYTHIC ENTRANCEMENT

One of your challenges will be to see what emerges if previous connections are abandoned and reconstructed with different links. Sometimes changing just a small detail can redirect the whole thrust of your story. The 1998 film Sliding Doors, for example, tells two completely different stories for the same two characters depending on whether one of the characters manages to catch a train or miss it.

Sometimes the challenge is simply introducing a different interpretation to a given situation. For example, the interpretation I put on my being 10 minutes late for a business appointment that led to the contract cancellation, for a number of years, impacted on my sense of competence and resulted in me doubting my abilities and no longer working in that particular sector. But, if I return to that story, what happens if I reinterpret it? That door being slammed shut in my face led directly to my starting to write (through recognising I'd been ignoring my voice of creativity). I don't regret that for a minute, so maybe that 10 minutes of my life, was a blessing in disguise and not a stain on my competence? That is a very liberating reframing of my story.

We have a tendency to apportion blame first, and usually on the nearest, most convenient recipient – ourselves – and there it remains anchored. We believe that once we can attach blame, we can move on, but that is rarely the case as blame leads to guilt and dissatisfaction.

The ways we establish links and maintain them are constructed on the basis of our habits, experiences and expectations, and they are heavily influenced by the society and the environment in which we are raised. The weight of societal expectations must not be under-estimated. We all do things because it is expected of us, not because we really want to, even though we know those expectations are often contrary to our wellbeing. (Long work hours is one example.)

One South American tribe looks at the outside world with complete amazement and pity because it sees us as hidebound by what it terms (in translation), Mythic Entrancement. By this they mean that we live in a trance, unable to recognise and therefore challenge the assumptions upon which our myth, our worldview, our paradigm is based. We walk around, they say, completely oblivious to the most important things about us, and are completely unable to interpret the world in any way that is not consistent with the explanations we have created: our myths. Their worldview (itself arguably a mythic entrancement) is nature- and seasons-based, and their vocabulary is similarly nuanced and rich in those areas. They are especially conscious of the fragility of the ecological balance and are incredulous that other cultures are unable or unwilling to recognise what for them is blatantly obvious: that we are part of the natural world, and what we do to the world, we do to ourselves.

The task you now face requires profound challenging of previous assumptions

The task you are now engaged upon is made all the more difficult because it requires profound challenging of previous assumptions and redrafting them into a new paradigm. Part of our mythic entrancement, according to those South Americans, is our propensity, in even the most horrible of situations, to reconfigure the facts and events to fit the myth that makes them bearable. This then allows these situations to be excised from our immediate consciousness.

How often at a dinner party, or over coffee, or even in the workplace do you hear people say, "I don't know how you put up with it!" And the ensuing comment is almost always (to the outsider, a blatant excuse): "I'm doing it for my kids," or, "I just need a couple more years on my CV before I move on," or even, "maybe it's my fault?"

That person has created a story that makes life bearable and that has enabled them to ignore the frustration, the humiliation, the damage that's being done. They're living in their Comfort Zone. One of the saddest examples of this comes in my work as a Magistrate when I sit on domestic abuse cases. So often the complainant – and it's usually a woman – will say, "Yes, he hit me. He slapped me. He made my lip bleed. But he doesn't mean it. He loves me really. He's always sorry." Any challenge to the status quo, and the Comfort Zone, is erased.

Why? Why do we put up with second best? A large part of it is because to move on creates uncertainty, stress and difficulties. Change challenges our sense of security, it raises fear and anxiety, so more often than not, it is resisted.

Change challenges our sense of security

In his philosophical treatise, *The Republic*, Plato uses the story of a group of prisoners who had spent their lives chained together in a cave. All they can ever see is a series of shadows flickering on the cave wall in front of them. Over a period of time these cave dwellers ascribe characteristics and stories to the shadows to make sense of the confusing reality they see. Then one day, one of the prisoners is freed. He ventures to the cave mouth and beyond. He meets the people, animals and objects whose forms he has previously seen only in projection on the wall. He learns that this 'reality' is vastly different and more complex than the paradigms they'd previously imagined. In his excitement he returns to tell the others what he has discovered. But, according to Plato's story, the prisoners find his talk far too disconcerting and he's rejected as disruptive and mad, finally being forced to flee for his life.

This is Mythic Entrancement in 3rd Century BCE Greece. It is an ever-present danger, as I can confirm from my own experience. I am an only-child, and many studies claim to identify the common characteristics of an only child: a predilection towards selfishness because the only child has never been forced to share toys with siblings; and a tendency to escape into a personal inner world that fosters unusual creativity and self-reliance. Born to working class parents and raised in a troubled part of an inner city, I won a place at a selective grammar school several miles away. That was my equivalent of Plato's character leaving the cave (symbolically, you understand). I now inhabited two completely different worlds. And in both I told a different story: to my peers around where I lived, my desperation to be accepted led to me claiming I'd been 'forced' to attend that school but that I was still the same kid whose father worked in the factory and later became a school caretaker. At school, however, where I was just as desperate to fit in, I constructed a different story: my interests were in drama and reading and so I told them my father helped manage a school's 'non-teaching staff'. In truth, I felt as if I truly fitted in neither world. I blamed my parents, especially since academically I struggled, and always languished in the nether regions of performance.

From that and much more I have created the story or myth of my childhood and how it explains or justifies who I am today, especially my less positive side. It can never be the whole story, but it has served me well in the past. But what if I were to look at those childhood events that I can remember in a new light? What happens if I take the photographs of my childhood and connect them in a different way? Then a different story emerges – one where I was made to feel special and secure because I wasn't constantly fighting for 'space' with siblings. One where my parents actually went to great lengths to stop me being over-dependent on them; and they went to equal lengths to protect me from the fact that money was often desperately short.

What if I adopt this different story that, with years of later experiences, helps me see things in a different light? How might that change my perception of me? Because that previous story was drafted in the angst and turmoil of my teens with a seriously-ill mother, a struggling, unpleasant academic environment, a religious idealism and a busy social and sporting life designed to fill every waking moment with anything other than reflection. But it has become a story that is limiting and self-serving. Rather than being a victim of my childhood, as in the 'old' version of the story, in the 'new' version I can now see myself as having fashioned those experiences into determination, resilience and a drive to make a difference in people's lives. I have a wonderful elderly relative in her nineties who regularly tells me she has no idea how I managed to make so much of myself and how proud she is! But it is still a part of my story that richly deserves reconsideration in later life.

HOW A BROKEN NOSE SHAPED MY LIFE

By the time you reach the rarefied atmosphere of CEO or MD – or of any kind of success, even early on in your life – you will have had considerable training and experience in constructing an effective story that values the retaining of composure, saying the right things and being 'on message' to use the current business lexicon.

In a business context, stories are used to construct a past from which you can learn salutary lessons as you move forward in your chosen career. They are often focused on cold, hard facts. They are synthetic to the extent that they are 'artificially' constructed in order to serve a particular message that needs to be conveyed and to put the best possible gloss on what might otherwise be a demoralising or discouraging interpretation.

Stories can also be valuable in deflecting attention. For example, one of my defining features is a rather large nose. It is a Hyson characteristic. It is also bent over to one side. These are hard, cold facts and not ones I normally consider, unless they become an issue with other people. But if the topic of noses happens to crop up in conversation (and believe me, it happens more often than you might think) I have developed the facts into a diversionary story along the following lines:

When I tell people I broke my nose twice in my teens – as a swimmer – I tend to get rather strange looks. It's not easy to break your nose swimming I think. There are other more likely sports: rugby, hockey, football, boxing...

In my teens I was a competitive swimmer in Nottingham. I belonged to a very good club: Midlands Champions, which for several years running was high in the National League tables. I entered my teens – well the testosterone-pumping teens anyway – full of ambition, drive, and anger, with all sorts of teenage emotions boiling away inside. I was proud to be in a good club.

The senior squad, which I'd just joined, was much admired by the younger six, seven and eight year-olds: we were the gods. And the Chief God was Alan Widdowson. I still remember his name; I still see what he looked like: 6'6" tall, shoulders as broad as a building, blond hair, and he was AN ENGLAND INTERNATIONAL! In breaststroke. My stroke. In my age-group. I can't tell you how many hours I spent watching his backside powering away from me down the lanes. He was my rival. So for several years my ambition was to beat Alan Widdowson.

I trained hard. I got better. Although Alan's rear end never seemed to get any nearer. Because of course, Alan trained. And got better.

Every Friday evening was club night for swimmers young and old. The senior squad was scheduled directly after the juniors so those youngsters could actually see what they could strive to be – the elite towering above them.

Before our session began we helped out with those younger club members, directed by their coach, so we could get to know them and they us.

When it came to their playtime we were called back to our serious business of the evening. Now of course you'll work out immediately that frolicking young children and powerful adolescents in full training are a potential health hazard in close proximity.

So the pool was divided into two at the halfway point. And we trained across the pool. In widths. Which is all very well until you realise that in the remaining 10 sessions of the week we trained in lengths. And so it was that one evening I, as a breaststroke swimmer, lost my sense of direction, opened my shoulders, pulled back my arms – and hit the wall. Nose first. And to prove it was no fluke a year or so later I did it again!

Which is how the gentle sport of swimming continues to affect my face four decades later.

So, there is a useful diversionary tactic in that story: I can justify my broken nose, and in the past it helpfully avoided me tackling an underlying issue – that of my perception of my body image.

What diversionary stories do you tell others and why are they memorable to you? Note these down for future reference.

VALUES AND VISION

In the next stage of your evolving story the Activities begin to concentrate on your core values. We then use them to construct your vision of the way forward. As part of that, I need to introduce what I call 'gateway terminology'. This refers to those terms that carry a value and significance beyond their simple function. They are words that are symbolic and hold great richness and diversity. They act as a window into what is going on deep inside.

There is a longer list of gateway terms in the Appendix of this book. In the context of this chapter, some key gateway terms are:

+ Alchemy
+ Belonging
+ Calling
+ Collaboration
+ Community
+ Destiny

* Fulfilment
* Gift
* Give back
* Greater good
* Higher Power/Purpose
* Humanity
* Inner harmony
* Innovation
* Inspire/ation
* Intuition
* Legacy
* Making a difference
* Meaning
* Mission
* Presence
* Purpose
* Something missing
* Soul
* Spirit/uality
* Vision
* Vocation
* Wisdom

ACTIVITY 4.1 – GATEWAY TO THE FUTURE
Timeline 7

Look back over your Timeline and Story. Which, if any, of these gateway terms or words have you used?

* Why?

* Why not?

* Select up to 5 words that particularly appeal to you and see how you might apply them to some of your Timeline events.

- What happens to your Story when you do this?

- What happens if you apply the word Wisdom to it?

- Where do you see wisdom arise, and if it doesn't, why do you think that is?

Be playful here – enjoy the process and look at your Story from as many different angles as possible.

INSPIRATION FROM EXPERIENCE

One of the most significant terms on that list is Inspiration. The word literally means, 'in-spirit'. Inspiration is what fires up your spirit and drives you forward with the power necessary to overcome hurdles and transcend difficulties. It is the source of your Vision. In fact, your Vision is the outward story of that inner inspiration. Inspiration is vital if you are to be an innovative leader in your business, and in every part of your fulfilled and satisfying life. If you didn't initially choose Inspiration as a gateway word, take another look at your Timeline with this as your key word. When were the times when you were most inspired? What caused that feeling? What circumstances initiate inspiration for you?

Vision, initially, seems totally beyond one's grasp. It's illusive and it may not come naturally. But my advice is to just recognise that when you start, you won't necessarily know how you will achieve your vision, or indeed what your vision might be. But trust this process because out of all the work you are doing, your new vision for the future will arise. Without it, you will never be able to leave the Desert of Transition.

Trust the process, and out of the work you are doing, your vision will arise

The next section features true case studies of two people – Mike Johnson and Neal Gandhi – both of whom have faced these same questions and drawn on their inspiration in order to find a way out of the Comfort Zone, through into the next stage, the Wilderness, and eventually determining their calling, their Legacy. A later section in this book will look at their outcomes.

Mike Johnson *spent twenty years rising up through BP Castrol culminating as Global Head of Castrol at BP. Castrol is a $9bn global lubricant business that has over 7,500 employees in 60 countries worldwide.*

One of the defining features of his leadership was that alongside business growth they focused on creating and developing global brands with an awareness of the importance of understanding cross-cultural differences. In his years with the company as Global CEO (2007-13) turnover grew from $7bn US to $9bn; profits grew from $250m in 2005 to $1.4bn in 2010, where they remained. For the first time, the company got involved in sponsorship (e.g. the Soccer World Cups of 2010 and 2014) and invested in premium brands to raise awareness. In China, brand awareness rose from 5% to 50%.

"Castrol," he says, "always took huge pride in its brand and having company-branded clothing underlined that. People were proud to wear it. It also emphasises that the company believes strongly in legacy."

His Vision at work was encapsulated in three readily-identified words: PROTECT (people); DEFEND (margins); and ATTACK (inefficiencies). This resulted in a huge turnaround in Castrol when it might easily have folded. The fact that Castrol lived on after his tenure is what he describes as his legacy and he is particularly proud that the 'people' element is still paramount.

After 40 years of working life, having left school at 16, Mike began feeling there must be 'something more to life'. This led to him leaving Castrol at the end of 2013 with several months 'gardening leave'.

Although he had been on the company's pre-retirement preparation programme, he had little idea of what he wanted to do other than travel and devote more time to his voluntary work. Further clarity came when a friend in Thailand told him that in that country, they see three distinct phases in life: Learning; Doing; Giving Back.

But 18 months on, he's starting to feel the need for a greater challenge and wishes he'd perhaps done that thinking a few years before ending his time with Castrol. He's missing the intellectual challenge, although he is involved in a portfolio of projects that include mentoring young people; being a Visiting Professor at the University of Sunderland; Chair of Trustees with SMASH (Swindon Mentoring and Self-Help); and a member of the Advisory Board for The Football Leagues Managers' Association.

Neal Gandhi *is what might be called a serial entrepreneur. He set up his first company, Jungle.com, at the age of 21 and sold it to Argos in 2000 in a £37m deal.*

Five years later, he sold his second company with earn-out (contingent payments) and four years after that, while still only 30 years old, he sold his third company to London's Tech City.

But his fourth company, in his own words "went to my head and I began to lose it." For a few years he enjoyed all the trappings of wealth, but as he now admits, he was using the material benefits to mask the gnawing thought that there must be more to life than this. "I was desperately searching while at the same time thinking, 'I can't stand the thought of building another four businesses until I'm 65!'"

Fed up with it all, he says he made a number of poor personal decisions that culminated in 2012 with his wife announcing she no longer loved him and that he must leave the marital home.

"For the first time in my life, that forced me to stop and take stock. The maximum time off I'd ever had previously was 3 weeks. It made me look around and realise, 'You've trashed everything you've ever cared for.'"

There will be more from both Mike and Neal in a later chapter.

One of the things that both Mike and Neal did to resolve their impasse, was to talk with a group of trusted people looking for their different insights and suggestions. I recommend you do the same. Your on-going Story is especially important here. Listeners are disadvantaged when all they are presented with is a long list of cold facts, a list of skills and/ or possible where-nexts. It is hard for them to get a feel for the true you – and even harder for them to feel motivated to go the extra mile to help. By the way, 'Story' here does not mean the superficial gloss put on a disaster to reframe it as a glowing success. It means the searingly honest warts-and-all version that you have been working on throughout the course of this book; the one that helps the listener feel they have a part to play in your success and therefore, the motivation to go the extra mile in doing so. If you give them the full-monty, they *want* to help. They will want to be part of the Third Act resolution of such a compelling drama. So, if you feel reluctant to share that level of honesty with the people you have in mind – they are the wrong people!

A word of caution here echoes something I have said before: when you share a problem, particularly if you are a man, usually your first and strongest reaction is the desire for your listener to solve it. This is because we live in a solutions-focussed environment. But, at this point that is not the contribution we are asking for. Their gift to you is to *listen*; to reflect back what they think you are saying and to help you get clarity. It is most definitely not to superimpose their solutions onto your questions. Nor, initially, is their role to prompt you to solutions at this stage either. That will come later.

You owe it to yourself to spend sufficient time in this stage to explore all the things you've discovered up to this point, and not to jump to premature commitments, however attractive they might seem.

WHAT STORIES DO YOU TELL?

It is quite likely that as part of this iterative, interactive process, you will begin to reframe or draft some parts of your Story. In fact, I would be rather disappointed if you didn't because it is highly unlikely you will get full insight and clarity in the first few iterations.

That is particularly the case with what we tend to call 'unfinished business': those events where there was an outcome that continues to feel unsatisfactory to us but where the events of the incident were and are beyond our control. If we cannot change the detail it can often help us to move on from it by reinterpreting how we view and describe it. Take the true story of Michael Pollan's Vernal Pool:

Pollan was inordinately proud of his new pond that he could see from his study window. It was guaranteed to calm his working day. He even wrote articles about it for The New York Times extolling how it had, "transformed a gaping wound in the earth into a thriving habitat giddy with life". Until it promptly emptied – and then a few months later, filled again. Despite many visits, consultancies, Internet searches and more, no-one could explain this annoying, regularly repeating process. Until he happened to mention it to an elderly local man who knew the problem instantly – the pond was located on a slope and built into rock, so it would constantly fill and empty: it was a vernal pool. Pollan could have continued literally pouring money into the project; he could have continued to rue the disappointment; or he could reframe his perception of it. And so it became, "a window on a seasonal underground river".

As part of the important process of reflection, in the next Activity I ask you to look back at your Timeline and Story and consider especially the time when you felt you were in-tune with life and riding high.

When you know things are going well, that is an indication there is sufficient alignment with what you need and want, compared to those things that drain your energy: we talk about this as being 'in the flow'. Here, you are identifying the flow of your life and then being in touch with that flow, which is itself in touch with the natural cycles or flows of life. This is synergy or interconnectivity.

ACTIVITY 4.2 – GOING WITH THE FLOW
Timeline 8

+ Now you are becoming clearer about the themes emerging from the Story of your life, go back and reframe some of your key events in this light.

+ Think about those where you feel you were at your best and where you got the most satisfaction from what you contributed.

+ It might help to concentrate on perhaps four of them, adding in as much detail and description as you can remember. What was it about these events that made you feel good?

+ Consider especially what the achievement was, how you came to get involved in it, what you actually did and what you found especially satisfying or enjoyable or encouraging about it.

Your overall Timeline is now developing multiple stories and outcomes. It is very useful to keep your options open as long as possible, because as you create different stories or versions of the same story you will notice that some generate more excitement and energy in you than others. Those are the ones pointing you towards something of enormous value.

SUMMARY

In this chapter you have:

+ Challenged and re-evaluated your mythic entrancement and diversionary stories that can mask the deeper story of your life.

+ Used some different 'gateway terminology' to review your story and particularly the importance of wisdom and inspiration.

- Considered the implications of deliberately reframing your story as with the vernal pool.

'Midway this way of life we're bound upon
I woke to find myself in a dark wood
Where the right road was wholly lost and gone.'

Dante Alighieri, Divine Comedy, Inferno

Chapter 5

CHALLENGING UNCONSCIOUS LIMITATIONS

Do those words of Dante's resonate with you? Perhaps 'the right road being wholly lost' was the trigger point for your current exploration? The journey into the 'dark wood' can come via many different paths. Sometimes it can be traumatic and beyond your control such as a bereavement, divorce, a deterioration in health, a business failing or an unexpected redundancy. Sometimes the path can begin with a positive and deliberate choice: feeling dissatisfied with your current job and resigning, confident that the next opportunity lies just around the corner, only to discover that just around the corner is the dark wood rather than the new dawn. Sometimes you might simply know you have to do something without ever having any clear idea what; you might even know that there will be a dark wood ahead but you understand that the only way into your new beginning must be by travelling through the dark wood. There are many others reasons why you might find yourself lost deep in that dark wood.

I should point out here that the darkness to which I am referring to is not that of psychological depression. That is a very different beast even if some of the preliminary features may be similar. So if these feelings are accompanied by an inability to get out of bed in the morning, or a significant loss of appetite; if you have serious problems with sleep accompanied by bouts of irritation or anger, reckless behaviour or self-loathing, it is time to seek some *medical* advice.

The 'dark wood', however you enter it, is a time of disorientation

The dark wood I refer to here, however you enter it, is a time of disorientation. As I wrote earlier, when you wake up in this darkness, one of the first things to strike you is the lack of any commonly recognisable or familiar landmarks, coupled with the limitations that the darkness places on your senses. You are only too aware that previous habits and ways of doing things no longer work now the first phase of life nears completion. Not only do they not work, they no longer prove satisfying. Indeed, you may well even be wondering how on earth you managed to stay with them for so long.

There is a further cause of entering the dark wood that is particularly relevant in the context of this book. Sometimes the darkness results from the *unconscious limitations* placed on you by yourself or by other people. These limitations may be a fear of failure that prevents you taking any next step in case it is the wrong one. Or it may be the limitation that fears success so that you are already predisposed to wreck an enterprise on the cusp of success. A similar limitation has sometimes been referred to as 'Imposter Syndrome': the fear that sooner or later 'they' will find out you are not as good as they think you are; that you have only been appointed or promoted because you are the token woman, the token member of another ethnic group, the only person willing to take the job... One of the biggest limitations comes from the habit of always seeing the negative or downside, the snags or complications rather than the opportunities. The list of limitations you might put on yourself is endless.

> ## One of the biggest limitations we place on ourselves comes from the habit of always seeing the negative or downside rather than the opportunities

In this chapter you have the opportunity to check whether there might be unconscious limitations that are holding you back from fulfilling your potential, the purpose for which you are being called. And if so, to offer some suggestions about how you might find the road that currently seems lost to you.

ACTIVITY 5.1 – SEEING THAT WHICH IS INVISIBLE

In Timeline 7 from the previous chapter we looked as some gateway words. Vision was among them.

- I would like you to go back to this Timeline and see if you included vision as one of your chosen gateway words.

- If not, I would like you to re-do the exercise using vision as the key word. The reason for this is that to challenge unconscious limiting beliefs, you have to be able to *see* or *envisage* beyond them; it's all about creating a new vision that comes from deep within you and that is not influenced by others. This may be the first time you've had the opportunity to remove these shackles.

• So, apply the word vision to some of the key events in your life and see how this changes or affects them. Where does vision arise for you?

• Reframe your story using vision and let it embed deep into your consciousness.

• Is there a key phrase or word that evolves, which links you to this new story? Such as, "*Trust the Vision that comes to me in times of focused work.*" Or, "*Remember my Vision to create a Mentoring scheme for my work team.*" If so, display it on your computer screen or work desk. Fix it with a magnet to your fridge. Frame it on a wall. Whatever it takes for this to be a constant reminder and, more powerfully, a constant energy generator. Use it to review your Timeline and Story and search out the times that have prepared you for the next stage of turning the vision into reality.

Then consider this quote by George Bernard Shaw:

"Some men see things as they are and say 'Why?' I dream of things that never were and say, 'Why not?'"

When I first worked through the activities presented in this book, I became aware of numerous different voices offering me conflicting opinions. One of the loudest and most persistent voices was that of my parents – or at least, my interpretation of their combined essence. They devoted much of their time, effort and very limited money to raising me and as I am an only child, they were also very clear about their expectations for me. They were determined that I should have the opportunities denied to them, my father in particular. Their voices were part of a cacophony trying to tell me how to live my life, often with the most laudable of intentions and perhaps significant wisdom and insight. But in later life, one of the things I have had to learn was that I can only live my own life, not other people's version of it. My answers to those activities have to be to my satisfaction, not anyone else's.

Which brings me on to a particularly important step, best introduced by way of an illustration.

The pike is a large freshwater fish whose favourite meal is the tiny minnow. If you put a pike in a large tank and add a few minnows the pike soon eats the minnows. However, if you then put a clear partition between the two, the pike will soon learn that it's there and give up. Then, even if the partition is removed and the minnows swim freely alongside the pike, it won't try to eat them. Eventually, the pike will even starve to death.

One of the necessary challenges in the dark wood is to look back at those partitions or unconscious limitations in your previous experiences that have become the forgotten barriers – and seek to remove them – otherwise, like the pike, you will be starved of inspiration.

Those invisible partitions are dangerous because they dramatically impact both personal and business life. For example, many business leaders will inherit teams where those 'partitions' have been deeply cemented in to the business culture over the years; it is easy for new managers to identify 'inexplicable' behaviours, but have no idea what past partitions or barriers have caused them. These partitions are the unwanted legacies of previous managers' decisions, styles, and attitudes that have been explicitly or implicitly rewarded. For example, one unit director who reported to me was very reluctant to take any decision or even implement any procedure without first checking with me: his emails were numerous and detailed and his telephone calls long and pedantic. However much I told him that he did not need to do this, nothing changed. Then finally I took him to one side for coffee and asked him to tell me more about himself and his career. I asked him about his experiences with his previous line manager and all became clear: he had been constantly criticised and felt himself undermined at every turn, and so he had learned to protect himself every step of the way and avoid taking initiatives. That was the barrier. He was completely unaware of this invisible partition. Once I could proactively find ways of taking him through the barrier, it ceased to be an issue.

At a personal level, the partition may be less obvious but the outcome is likely to be equally limiting and debilitating. These may include...

- Fear, especially that chaos will ensue: the chaos of the unknown, the uncertain or the things you cannot control. This is a real struggle for many people. Yet the key is that the demolition of this particular partition comes through regularly reminding yourself and reinforcing the fact that *true creativity can only emerge from chaos, from dismantling.* It reminds me of the theosophical quote: "Only through destruction do you get creation." This is not about the artist stripping back part of a painting that they are dissatisfied with in order to paint it again in a hopefully improved version. It is about the artist grabbing a completely new, blank canvas. This is not to say that some aspects of the old painting cannot appear in the new, and inevitably, the painting will be enriched or limited by the skill of the artist – but, it is nonetheless a blank canvas surrounded by potential.

- The past voices of parents, siblings or other family members, or the school bully, either teacher or pupil may still haunt you. Or perhaps an undermining manipulative spouse or partner has created barriers and limitations that you feel you cannot cross? These voices echoing across the decades from childhood to now, telling you that you can never be good enough, or worthy enough, or clever enough, have got to go. Even if it had been true, that was then – this is now. Now you are a different person and are successful, however you define that. So these invisible partitions needs to go.

True creativity can only emerge from chaos

ACTIVITY 5.2 – TEAR DOWN THE WALLS

As you scan back over both your Timeline and Story, where are those partitions or limiting beliefs?

+ In whose voice do they speak?

+ How will you now remove them?

+ If you act on George Bernard Shaw's dictum of 'Why not?' what difference will it make to your plans?

These questions are of particular relevance to Jim Preston. He is responding to a question from his coach:

"What was I passionate about as a teenager? Rugby. You wouldn't believe it but I was actually pretty good. County standard, in fact. I loved the physical contact but also the fact that after the match, we'd all share a beer together in the clubhouse. I enjoyed the discipline and respect; the adrenalin and competition. In fact, I stood down from the first team to captain the second team – because I loved that responsibility. It was my first taste of leadership. It was addictive. And when my body started to protest too much, that's when I moved into coaching the youngsters."

Jim stares out the window reminiscing. In the chair opposite, Chris waits in silence, taking the opportunity to study him more closely.

He's struck by how much Jim's face has softened during that speech. His shoulders have straightened and the thought strikes Chris that actually, Jim would have been quite a formidable opponent.

"Anyway, that's all in the very dim and distant past."

"Was there anything else you were passionate about at that time?"

"Apart from playing for England?"

"Well, what inspired you at that time?"

"Good question... I guess I was something of an idealist at university. I went on various protest marches – Greenpeace, anti-apartheid, that sort of thing. The naivety of thinking I could change the world."

"And now...?"

"Oh now I'm much more the realist."

"And what's your worst fear in all this?"

"Hmm, that's a hard one..."

"Okay, I'll make some more coffee while you think about that one."

Once more Jim gazes out the window, more than a little disconcerted by the knot that has grown in his stomach. He grabs his pen and scribbles half a dozen words, then spins lines off from them to other words already on the page. Then he raises an eyebrow and resumes his out-of-the-window stare.

"How are you getting on, Jim?"

He jumps slightly: when did Chris come back in? "That was such a good question. The thing I'm most afraid of is being obsolete and ending up on the scrapheap. Like watching the train pull out of the station without me on board."

Chris nods. "That sounds like a limiting belief. So here's the challenge. Where might that same fear show itself in your past? And where might it have held you back or pushed you in a particular direction?"

The real iniquity of these limitations is in their impact. They not only reinforce a negative belief, but they also reinforce an inaccurate self-belief.

ACTIVITY 5.3 – WHY YOU WERE BORN

What is the *second most important day in your life*? This is not a trick question! In fact it is one of the most important questions in this book. Author Richard Leider frequently asks people this question. (The most important day in your life, he says, is the day you were born.) His answer is: the day you realise why you were born. The question 'why?' and its theme of challenging what you have done so far and what you will do in the next phase of your life is the key characteristic of this transition zone, this wandering in the wilderness or the dark wood.

This is because at some level, you have now become aware of the necessity to answer this question: why was I born? What was I put on this earth to achieve? What was I put here to leave behind? Where will I have made a positive difference? To answer these questions, the first thing to do is to remove those unconscious limitations that have been an insurmountable chasm preventing you from moving on to that next phase. The next thing is to evaluate your Timeline using the process below:

- I want you now to evaluate what is the 'Second Most Important Day in your Life', and determine from that what you were put on this earth to achieve, and therefore, what your legacy may be. This is perhaps the hardest exercise in this book so far, so do not rush it. Take your time and reflect and revisit this question until you feel you have pinpointed this.

- The second most important day in your life is the day you realise why you were born; it is the day where you discover the gift that is uniquely yours to give. So go back carefully over your Timeline and see if you can discover that day. Was it the day your husband booked you in to a writing course? Was it the day you realised that you loved building things (houses, businesses, implements…)? Was it the day you realised you wanted to be a teacher?

◆ Once you can answer this question you will know how you can make a difference. You will have a clear vision for the future and you will be inspired to achieve it. And, you will know what resources you will need to draw on.

One final unconscious limitation that you might experience currently comes in the form of feeling no-one else fully understands what you are currently wrestling with (which might well be true amongst your family, friends, acquaintances and business associates but most certainly is not on the wider scale); and that the whole experience is random, uncharted and hostile territory. The feeling is that once the road is lost and gone (as in Dante's 'dark wood') then that must mean the wood itself is uncharted and unknown.

In fact the dark wood is often simply a process of change, admittedly where the old familiar landmarks have disappeared, but nevertheless it is not unknowable. One of the first people to notice that in times of shock people seem to go sequentially through a series of stages, was Elisabeth Kübler-Ross. Her model related particularly to post-bereavement steps but can be triggered by most crises and times of major upheaval including moving house or losing a job. (See Appendix.)

The following sequence was developed to show some of the common stages people go through immediately after retirement but might also be relevant to you if you have recently left behind a business you founded or in which you invested significant effort and commitment, especially if it feels like your 'baby'. Typically, these phases of retirement or withdrawal begin with the **honeymoon period** where you experience the new joys of freedom, extra time to devote to things you consider important and with the resources to dedicate to them; this stage can quite quickly (within a few months) be replaced by feeling **disorientation** because all the familiar signposts have gone, such as the time to go to work, the purposefulness of achieving something and the fact that you can no longer describe yourself to others in terms of your work, of what you 'do'. This can be followed by a period of **disenchantment**: you miss people you used to see daily, there is a limit to the time you can spend on holiday reading or sunbathing, and it is not all it was cracked up to be or indeed, that you dreamed it would be. Then comes a time of **reorientation** as new signposts are created: perhaps the monthly dinner with old colleagues or the emergence of a new hobby or even the seizing of a new and unexpected business opportunity. This re-establishes **stability** and finally a returning sense of normality in the changed circumstances. (This idea is covered more fully in Hopson & Scally's excellent book *The Rainbow Years*.)

Different people will spend different periods of time in each stage or even pass through them almost unnoticed. If the period of change has been brought about by circumstances beyond your control and is unwelcome, then it commonly takes longer to pass through the dark wood of disorientation or disenchantment. Some will even pass through some of the stages more than once. But the path through the wood is both chartered and navigable.

ACTIVITY 5.4 – LOOKING FOR PATTERNS
Timeline 8

- Look back at your Timeline and life Story. When you were at your most successful and least successful – what were you doing?

- When your energy was at its highest, what were you doing? (Apply the gateway terminology here.)

- Neuropsychology asks: What are the patterns? What has brought you to this point? Which patterns will continue to serve you moving forward? What new ones will you find? How will you use these to maintain and fuel your inspiration?

- Where else might you seek help? Who do you know in your networks, for example?

SUMMARY

In this chapter you have had the opportunity to:

+ Identify your unconscious limitations and how to dismantle those partitions or barriers.

+ Recognise that the transition zone of the 'dark wood' may feel like a solitary wilderness, but is actually chartered territory and you can use your Story to navigate it successfully.

+ Evaluate what is the Second Most Important Day in your Life and determine from that what you were put on this earth to achieve, and therefore, what your legacy may be.

"The master in the art of living makes little distinction between his work and his play, his labour and his leisure, his mind and his body, his education and his recreation, his love and his religion. He hardly knows which is which. He simply pursues his vision of excellence at whatever he does, leaving others to decide whether he is working or playing. To him he is always doing both."

(Zen Buddhist Master)

CHAPTER 6
WHAT DO I WANT TO ACHIEVE?

The first chapters of this book concentrate on framing a vision and looking back at your life in order to help you identify your key values, habits and inspirations; to see where doors have been closed and to consider when and where you have been at your best. They have stressed the importance of making new connections, associations and interpretations.

The focus in the remaining chapters moves to the future: using what you know and have learnt about yourself, and especially your vision and values to create a future that will both stretch and develop your talents, generate energy, enable you to make a positive difference and then establish your legacy. These chapters will warn against some blind alleys or distractions and recognise there may be times and opportunities to test and experiment before the final clarity comes.

In much the same way that Millennials and Gen X/Y have new and different expectations from both life at work and life beyond work, the same is true at the opposite end of the spectrum with the commonly-called Baby Boomers – a generation that has already enjoyed a raft of opportunities and freedoms never previously available, including freedom from:

- Geographical constraints: as families become more scattered and worldwide travel ever easier, there is unprecedented choice over location including the countries in which we choose to work.

- Debilitating illness and its effects.

- Age stereotyping especially the assumption that by 65 we are no longer able to work.

One of the most important tasks of leadership is imagining (i.e. image-ing or image-making) a future that does not yet exist. Great leaders have the ability to imbue their ideas with vision, values and aspirations – and then breathe life into them so that they inspire others. (The Greek root for both vision and aspiration is *pneumos* meaning to breathe life into something.)

What will it take for you to claim your own freedom?

Does your vision inspire you? Does it breathe life into you? When you share it with others does it throb with energy, figures of speech, symbols, metaphors…? Does it excite them as well as you? Does it fill you with powerful determination that will drive you to overcome hurdles and be a magnet to others? If not, then there is further work to be done on it and I would advise you to revisit Activity 5.1.

What will it take for you to claim your own freedom and to create the balanced life of your own choosing?

Please note: some of these questions are deliberately ambiguous; they mean what you want them to mean. If your personality wants to scream and run a mile at this imprecision, bear with me. The whole purpose of this book is to invite you to try new ways of tackling things.

Some people conduct this search as if it were another business project. That is, they consult, plan, research, investigate, question, speculate, and undertake a risk analysis. There's nothing wrong with that – except here I am inviting you to dream, to let your imagination have free reign and undertake that process of re-image-ing your future: to breathe life into it.

VOCATION

To talk about having a vocation, a calling, may seem a little pretentious, and best suited to medics, teachers and the religious who really do make a difference to people's lives. Not so. Most definitions of vocation refer to some sort of calling: *that which you cannot help but do*. Sometimes it can be a calling *from*; sometimes it can be a calling *to*. Either way, there is an implication that something greater than 'just me' is involved: that there is another voice apart from my own. Some people refer to this as a 'higher power' drawing them on.

Vocation: that which you cannot help but do

This calling or vocation never asks you to become something you are not; it always calls you to be the fullest version of who you are: your complete self. Parker (*Let Your Life Speak* – listening for the voice of vocation. 2000, p25) describes it as "something I can't not do, for reasons I'm unable to explain to anyone else and don't fully understand myself, but are nonetheless compelling." That is where vocation differs from vision: vocation might be something you could never really explain to anyone else, you just know it is there; vision is how you begin to bring vocation into reality, something you will focus on that will compel you forward. This is not a cheap motivational carrot dangled just out of reach. It is an internal prompting voice. The gift of who we were when we first arrived – the true self as Palmer calls it.

SIGNATURE STRENGTHS

In previous chapters I encouraged you to identify the things that you most enjoy doing: then I took this a stage further and invited you to identify the things that you are particularly good at; your skills or gifts, the things that make you stand out from the crowd. (These are what American psychologist Martin Seligman, calls 'signature strengths'.) You may only have two or three signature strengths but they are of supreme importance because they not only set you apart from other people and constitute the pillars on which you have built your life to date, but they also need to be part of the future you construct. They are integral to you and without them you cannot completely be your true self.

That does not necessarily mean they need to be part of your work: they might be exercised in a hobby, club or volunteer activity. Some of the most fulfilled, inspiring leaders are found coaching Junior League or running teams of volunteers in hospices or in countries with emerging economies.

ACTIVITY 6.1 – MAKING CONNECTIONS

In your notepad, describe an occasion when you have felt especially connected to the world around you; when you have felt drawn or compelled towards a particular decision or course of action.

+ What does that begin to show about your mission in life?

+ What in your life are you most proud of? Why?

THE INTEGRATED LIFE

Ask any busy employer and they will tell you that one of the biggest issues they face is the rapidly increasing number of work days lost through stress – and a significant part of this flows from the difficulty many workers face aligning their existing priorities with their deepest beliefs and values.

You may deliberately choose to ignore that misalignment for a period of time, for example working excessive hours for a few years in order to achieve future success which will give you more time with family. You may need to do so in order to build your business to some future point in time when it will all be different, and you'll have enough money to do what you want. Or, you may be aware of the mismatch at some level but choose not to consider the implications. But sooner or later that misalignment will surface. While you may deliberately choose delayed gratification, the resulting energy-draining position can only be maintained for a limited period without suffering significant damage. You were not designed to operate out of balance for long periods at a time.

At the point when the things that have previously brought you success or satisfaction no longer do so, there is a gap, and somehow whatever you try more of, fails to fill it. When that happened to me a few years ago I spent some time with a therapist exploring what was going on. I had spent years as an independent business consultant, I had a good list of clients and enjoyed a positive reputation. But of course I had to go where the work was and when it came I grabbed it with both hands because there was never any guarantee when the next work would come along, or even if it would. The result was working long hours either delivering the business or else chasing after business or building networks. The quality of my sleep dropped and dreams were frequent, usually about missing train connections or being lost and feeling out of control. The key moment came when my therapist said, "Peter, you're a creative person. But you've been ignoring it for years. This is your creative voice wanting to be heard once more."

For me the integration at that moment was not about whether I should work less and have more recreation; that would not pay the bills or keep my business afloat. No, my imbalance was about what deep and intrinsic part of myself was being neglected and needed acknowledging and bringing back into the balance. I needed to build that in to what I was already doing. There was a persistent but ignored inner voice. That was the point at which I began creative writing and started work on my novel. Very soon it was generating significant new energy and satisfaction and continues to do so. It enabled me to become a cultural creative and restore something that had been smothered since my teens. My life had a little more integration and balance.

An 'Integrated Life' is actually quite a complex thing to achieve. Given that a web search for Work/Life Balance yields in excess of 50 million links, it is also obviously of widespread interest and concern.

Author and businessman Stephen Covey summed up the fundamental aspirations of a balanced and fulfilling life as: Live, Love, Learn and Leave a Legacy.

Achieving an Integrated Life is a little like riding upon a see-saw: it requires constant work to avoid suddenly finding yourself catapulted into the air, only to land in pain and confusion with an almighty crash! And many are the weights queuing up to descend from a great height to land on the opposite side of your see-saw and catapult you off balance. A see-saw requires a pivot against which to balance. If you can find that, then your chances of maintaining some equilibrium are immeasurably greater.

BUT it is also worth pointing out that complete balance results in complete inertia and that is not much fun either! An Integrated Life is not so much about perfect balance as about being able to choose the appropriate balance at any given time and feel you have control over it rather than it controlling you (sometimes referred to as Time Sovereignty). The areas of balance that need to be fine-tuned are: Body, Heart, Mind and Soul (or Spirit) – roughly equating to Covey's Live, Love, Learn and Legacy. We need to nurture each of these aspects of our self, because where one is under-developed, the impact is like a chair with one or more shorter legs.

Balancing the needs of the body, heart and mind, with that of the soul, is one of the struggles facing our story character, Diya:

Diya collects her notes together on the lectern then takes a moment to glance around at the two hundred or so people clapping their hands in appreciation. Her talk seems to have been well received, and why not? She's given them what they wanted: a little bit of the fairy-tale local-girl-makes-good; a little bit of the realist long hours, stress and risk; and a little bit of the inspirational you-too-can-do-it. And as far as she could judge, none had spotted her performance-stopping crisis realisation, that she'd covered by simply pausing, looking around and nodding until she regained momentum. She turns and walks off stage still high on the adrenalin.

Only some hours later as the after-effects of the adrenalin high wear off, does she remember that dreadful moment. Even now her heart misses a beat at how close she came to disaster. The blankness felt as if it lasted for ten minutes but she knows it could only have been seconds. But how did it happen? She'd been fully on top of her notes; the delegates had laughed mostly in the right places and seemed to be attentive...

She scans through her script and finally locates the rough point she'd reached. At first it seems uncontroversial: talking about selling her third company and realising she could now do pretty much whatever she wanted in life with that level of financial security. Then she realises it was her ensuing hypothetical question to her audience – "what next?" And her response: "that means I've got time for at least three more!" that floored her. It should have filled her with excitement, after all, how can you inspire your audience if you don't feel inspired yourself? But she doesn't. That's precisely it. Another thirty years of doing this? No thank you. There must be something more, she thinks. But what? Definitely not the family business – I'd rather carry on as I am than do that! And the sooner everyone understands that the better.

Which is why, three days later, she is sitting across the table from her mentor Surinda Lakille in the local coffee shop. As he queues at the counter selecting his favourite chocolate caramel ("best in the city by a mile") she makes the conscious effort to be the calm, rational Diya who has forged so many successful negotiations.

"Surinda, I need your advice again."

He's only half way back from the counter, but is wise enough to simply raise an eyebrow and settle down into the brown leather chair opposite.

"Let me bring you up to date so you can see why I need your help. You know I've just sold the business? Well that means that I've finally got the financial security I've always wanted. I never need to work another day in my life, if I live carefully. I can do what I want. Or, I could carry on doing the same thing I've always done. I'm very good at it and I've already got a queue of companies as long as my arm begging me to invest. But do you know what? I'm bored with it. I want a new challenge. I know there's something out there, something I need to do. But I have no idea what."

"So what's brought this about?"

"I was speaking at a Conference just after I sold the business, telling them how wonderful it is to be an entrepreneur and I suddenly realised I didn't feel that anymore."

"Anything else?"

"No, I don't think so."

"Really?"

"Well, I've been under pressure to take over the family business. But there's no way on earth I'm going to do that!"

"I thought your father ran that? He's not retiring is he?"

"No – he died a few weeks ago. Now everyone thinks I should be the dutiful daughter and drop everything to come running back to help them out. My uncle emails me almost every day reminding me of my duty. And my brother's nearly as bad – I reckon he's scared stiff *it'll fall to him if I don't do it. They just don't understand I've built my own life, and it's not theirs to order about at will. I just know there's something else – something I need to do – but I've no idea what it is."*

"Is it such an unreasonable request? If you look at it from the perspective of the family and the business – is it a reasonable request?'

"...Yes. From their perspective, but not from mine." *She folds her arms and juts out her chin in defiance.*

"Then why not? What are you afraid of?"

"Afraid of? Absolutely nothing." *She realises she's raised her voice when several heads turn in their direction.* "It's just that I'd finally realised there was something missing in my work when Dad died. And I absolutely do know it isn't the family business."

"So what is it?"

"I don't know...! Something that enables me to give back, to use my business skills and all I've learnt to make a difference. All I need to do is find out what! Actually, I'm much clearer about what it isn't. It's certainly not about giving it all up and going off to live in some remote ashram or desert island. That most definitely isn't my vocation."

"That's a great point, Diya. It sounds like you will only be happy once you find your true vocation. So how would you describe what a vocation is?"

"No idea. People talk about teaching, nursing – but don't we all have some sort of vocation, something we're called to do?"

'Absolutely right. I once heard it described as 'whatever it is we can't avoid doing'. So I want you to think about the answers to three questions. Firstly, what makes you excited, what gives you energy? This will signpost your particular gifts, your signature strengths and you've been given those for a reason. When you use them, not only are you successful but you also inspire others. Secondly, what do you want to achieve? And thirdly, what won't you give up – at any cost? Oh, and one more: what do you fear in all this?"

Diya taps rapidly on her tablet device, noting down all these questions.

"But there's something else."

Her heart misses a beat and she glances up at him, catching the warning in his voice.

"You need to spend some time exploring what's going on between you and your family. You have more freedom than your parents or any previous generation – but therefore also more obligations. Now you need to look at the stories you've built up about your family – what you might call your family's mythology or folklore, especially around your father. We all connect family events by a narrative that we tell ourselves at the time in order to make sense of them. The trouble is, we don't often revisit them or check them out with others. And sometimes when we do that we make different connections so that a very different story emerges."

"How on earth will that help me find out what I'm being called to do? Sounds like a load of navel-gazing to me."

"Just trust me, Diya. When you've answered those questions, you'll find what it is that you and you alone are called to do. But be warned: this might take some months – it's not an overnight thing because you're reviewing a lot of things you've taken for granted for a very long time. So I suggest you write it all down, perhaps as the story of your life. And don't worry; nobody else needs to see it unless you choose to show it."

Had it been anyone else telling her to do these things, there is no doubt Diya would have laughed it away. But Surinda has been wise and right too often to be dismissed so readily. Although, had she known how long it would take, how difficult and challenging it would prove and how dark at times the journey would be, she might just have accepted the temptation to dismiss it.

REDEFINING LEADERSHIP

Generally, although not by any means exclusively, the calling to legacy and making a difference will involve you in some form of leadership capacity. It is my observation that for people going through this time of personal transition, there is often a corresponding change in their leadership style, which emerges with what I can only describe as more depth or colour and with a subtle change in focus that mirrors their change of emphasis.

It is too simplistic to see it merely in terms of moving away from primary profit-driven motives towards altruism. Perhaps it is best described as viewing and operating from a higher perspective and hence a broader perspective. It is my contention that just as the context in which you exercise leadership is changing (with the impact of Millennials; with changing expectations across the workforce and society as a whole; with rising expectations about corporate responsibility and ethical practices; and greater scrutiny or accountability), so is the very *essence* of leadership itself. This is partly the result of a growing awareness of emotional intelligence, but also because the mindsets, drivers and values of different generations in the workplace are all changing radically.

You are unlikely to have got to this point in your life without having both received and given leadership, whether that has been good or bad, healthy or damaging, at work or in a sports team, faith community, voluntary society or hobby. And the outcome of your current deliberations – your future direction – is likely to entail a reconsideration of what you mean by leadership and the exercise of it.

The best leaders have gone through what you are currently experiencing

People come into leadership via many different routes. You may have set up your own business as a sole trader or with a friend and then suddenly one day found yourself with a staff of five, then twenty, then fifty and with radically different expectations and demands on your leadership. You may have worked your way up the corporate ladder from team member to team leader to manager to director and beyond. You may have never exercised a formal leadership role but still found that people naturally gravitate to you to provide a lead. Whatever the route, the likelihood is that the next stage of your life will involve significant leadership, and it may require a very different style to anything you have used before. One of the biggest tragedies of business is the number of leaders who still think there is only one style of leadership and, even worse, that it is theirs!

I believe that all the best leaders have gone through what you are currently experiencing and that their 'greatness', their wisdom, has been forged in and by that very process. I sincerely believe this will be a huge part of your gift.

Mentoring is so important – except that here I mean the young mentoring the elders

You certainly do not need me to remind you that what is meant by leadership and how it is exercised continues to change rapidly. One of the biggest challenges for leaders is how to deal with the differing expectations and how to motivate an increasingly diverse workforce spanning Millennials and Gen X through to re-energised and powerful Baby Boomers often with an age range of half a century between them. It is necessary to learn from them in a way that no previous generation of leaders has had to – because the balance of power will no longer be with you but with them, especially Millennials. You will contribute the experience and the wisdom; they will contribute the power and the responsibility. They know it is ultimately up to them to create the future they want.

That is why mentoring is so important – except that here I mean the young mentoring their elders. If you are able to set the example by allowing younger staff to mentor you, to listen to them and allow them to help formulate your views this will be an important part of the story you are creating and will be a great example to others. Doing this will mark you out as a true leader and one who is already heading into the realm of legacy.

ACTIVITY 6.2 – YOUR LEADERSHIP QUALITIES

One of the huge advantages of taking this time to reflect, is to consider what sort of leadership characteristics you want to embody as you move forward.

- In light of this, what would you say is the outstanding leadership characteristic of your second phase of life, that is to say, in the point up until this transition?

- Does it tally with the leadership qualities you want to elicit in your legacy?

- If not, why not?

- Note these reflections down on your Timeline or in your notebook.

LEADERSHIP STYLES AND STAGES

Can outstanding leadership be learnt? Well, whilst it is true that outstanding leadership is often accompanied by an innate charisma, it is certainly possible to learn some *skills* of leadership; to improve by practice, reading books, attending courses and observing others. But the essence of *outstanding* leadership flows from the exercise of character.

At some point in your career to date, you have probably encountered 'old style' leadership from a generation that exercised it as command and control: "I say, you do." The movies caricature this as, "When I say 'jump', you ask 'how high?'"

Over the past thirty years that has largely been replaced by a more collaborative and consultative style. And alongside this has been the prominence of the charismatic or magnetic leader: the one that people instinctively feel drawn to following. Often those leaders do not even realise why that is the case; they do it instinctively and seemingly effortlessly.

Bill Torbert (Action Inquiry Leadership) argues that there are seven transformations and progressions of leadership:

1   Opportunist (5%);

2   Diplomat (12%);

3   Expert (38%);

4   Achiever (30%);

5   Individualist (10%);

6   Strategist (4%); and

7   Alchemist (1%:)

The leadership style with characteristics closest to those being discussed in this book – the style that most probably resonates with you – is the Alchemist. For example, they are unhurried in the midst of busy-ness; charismatic; aware of their own impact; and have high moral standards that focus strongly on truth.

Alchemist Leaders are particularly skilled in creating stories and metaphors that speak to people's hearts and minds. Mahatma Gandhi chose the symbol of a simple spinning wheel to advocate the values of nonviolent resistance to the dominance of the British Empire in India. He transformed the seething anger of the downtrodden into a movement for political change, based on nonviolent civil disobedience. In doing that he demonstrated clearly that he was an Alchemist Leader.

Alchemists have a clear vision based on what they feel called and driven to do and are determined that it will be their legacy. They have a strong awareness of Emotional Intelligence but go

a stage further because of their sense of vocation or calling –
they are what Maslow called self-transcenders.

I have focused on the Alchemist Leader not because they are
the only type of effective leader – clearly they are not – but
because they best epitomise the characteristics at the heart of
the current search you are embarked upon. They are the ones
most likely to be committed to transitioning to their legacy.
In story-writing terms they are the hero, the idealised person
we aspire to.

Alchemist Leaders are important for another reason. They
are representative of an emerging fourth intelligence: that of
spiritual intelligence.

ACTIVITY 6.3 – SYMBOLS OF TRANSFORMATION

In the light of Gandhi and Nelson Mandela (as detailed in
Chapter 1) skilfully using symbolism to forge a path into legacy,
I would like you now to reflect again on your Story or Timeline.

- Where you have pinpointed elements of inspiration and
  clarity in the above activities, such as in 5.1, try to picture
  a symbol that encapsulates that dream. For example, if you
  had a vision of starting a school for entrepreneurs, you may
  like to use a rosette to symbolise the goal.

- Think of it as you might approach developing a new logo for
  a business. The symbol should resonate with your vision.

- Sprinkle these symbols (there may be more than one)
  throughout your Timeline, wherever there is a convergence
  of energy or vision that links to your legacy.

Over the past two decades, much attention has been given
to the significance of *Emotional* Intelligence, whereby we
understand our own reactions and begin to learn how to manage

and develop them. Spiritual Intelligence (literally Spiritual Quotient as in IQ) is characterised by a sense of feeling 'called' by something external to oneself; to do something that is for the greater good. It is rooted in the third part of life, the stage where, once we emerge from the dark wood, we are aware of where we are heading and why.

SQ is the intelligence with which we access our deepest values, purposes and higher motivations. It is where our moral intelligence resides, giving us an innate ability to distinguish right from wrong. It is the intelligence with which we exercise goodness, truth, beauty and compassion. (Zohar & Marshall, 2004. *Spiritual Capital: Wealth We Can Live By*)

More specifically, Spiritual Intelligence – SQ – is about how people connect the activities of their daily life with their desire for meaning and to relate that to something greater than, and external to, themselves. It is "what compels us beyond ourselves and our narrow self-interests.... to make a difference." (Thompson, 2000, *The Congruent Life: following the inward path to fulfilling work and inspired leadership*.)

SQ is not about religion, though it is to do with the recognition of something outside of and greater than ourselves that has a pull or an attraction or even a claim on us. That it why it is called 'spiritual' intelligence.

You can probably look back and identify your preferred style of leadership without too much trouble. You may recognise times when it has served you well and times when it has not, and you have probably used different styles of leadership in different contexts. I am firmly of the opinion that leadership needs to be contextual. The leadership type to be exercised is the one selected to sit on the tripod of: 'at this time'; 'in this context'; 'with these resources'. That is why the burial ground of CEOs is littered with the epitaphs of those recruited from one organisation because of their outstanding record of success, only to sink without trace in the next: they and their Boards paid little attention to context. However, as a Spirited Leader, one who transforms and alchemises, you will have no such 'partitions' or boundaries in your thinking, because you have transcended them.

ACTIVITY 6.4 – DREAM A LITTLE DREAM

Sleep is not only about physical rest and regeneration. Psychoanalyst Donald W. Winicott described dreaming as the use of imagination to explore scenarios where your potential can come to fruition. Dreams allow your inner spirit, your soul, to unfurl.

Sleep allows the brain to process things that it has not been able to do during the course of the day. In sleep, the left brain, the part dealing with reason and logic, does not function because for it to do so requires us to be alert and conscious. So only the right brain, the part dealing with creativity, operates during sleep. Which is why some people claim that their best ideas come while they're asleep.

Most people can remember at least something of their dreams.

- If you are one of those, make a note of some of your recent dreams.

- If they are allowing your inner spirit or soul to unfurl, what are those dreams trying to tell you?

- What insights do they give about what you might be called to do?

- If they left you feeling uncomfortable, what might they be telling you to avoid?

ACTIVITY 6.5 – THE FILM OF YOUR LIFE

As I have stated above, it's always good to dream, so let's conflate your dream with your legacy here.

+ If there were to be a film of your life, what would be the storyline of the *next stage* going into the future?

+ I realise you don't really know yet – so be creative. Sketch out a few options and then see which ones excite you most.

+ What genre would it be? Drama? Tragedy? Comedy? Sci-fi?

+ What would it be called?

+ Why would people come to see it?

SUMMARY:

In this chapter, the first in the new, forward-looking section, you have had the opportunity to:

+ Clarify your vision and consider your vocation: that which you cannot *not* do.

+ Identify your 2 or 3 signature strengths to make sure they constitute a key element of your future planning.

+ Try and envisage your legacy symbolically.

+ Consider the impact of your styles of alchemy-leadership as you begin to focus on making a difference.

+ Look at your dreams and see if they are pointing you in any particular direction.

+ Identify any times when you have felt compelled or drawn to a particular course of action and to project that forward into the film of your life past and future.

"If you don't have any shadows you're not in the light."

– Lady Gaga

"You need to spend time crawling alone through shadows
to truly appreciate what it is to stand in the sun."

– Shaun Hick

CHAPTER 7

IDENTIFYING THE SHADOWS

everal years ago, I decided I could no longer put off the
daunting task of sorting out my family photographs.
I've been in houses where every single photograph is
documented and filed in labelled albums: holiday; family;
1999 etc. Mine were filed: in three boxes labelled 'Photos'! So
I decided to at least sift them according to decades, starting
with the earliest ones of my parents in the 1930s. The upshot
is that several hundred photographs now sit in smaller folders,
though still unmounted and unlabelled. More significantly,
the sifting revealed some absolute gems: my grandmother
staring imperiously at the camera in what I can only describe
as full Victorian splendour despite it being at least the 1920s;
special moments when my children were growing up. And one
that sparked a remarkable chain of events leading to quite a
revelation about what has made me who I am: a photograph
showing me at about the age of five posing with a group of other
five year-olds in front of a playhouse 'shop'. Clearly very early
school days. We are all smiling and clutching a variety of props:

dolls, cuddly toys, a broom, and I'm clutching a wheelbarrow. But that is not what struck me.

What I noticed with great amusement was that I was wearing a tie. Five years old, at school and unique in the photo, I was wearing a tie. But an even greater surprise lay in store. As I separated out the photos for that decade in my life, in every single one I am wearing a tie. Yes, there is even one of me on the beach wearing a tie while building a sandcastle! My parents had a very clear idea of what was 'proper' and smart in public. I have no recollection of how that was greeted by the other children or their parents, but as I grew up in quite a poor working class area of Nottingham, I suspect it may not have been entirely positive. It was likely to be viewed as a symbol of pretentious aspiration by my parents or of patronising pity towards me.

Could this ubiquitous tie wearing have any relation to the fact that for a long time I was considered quite straight-laced and formal? I suspect it could! As it happens, I grew much less formal as my twenties progressed but under pressure, elements of that straight-laced former self may still return. A shadow remains, one that is more prominent in the darker times than in the more enlightened periods of my life.

SHADOWS AND EFFECTS

When I look at events that have happened to me and see them in a new light, either intentionally or as a result of revelation, I reframe that story. That reframing may be as simple as recognising that I was a habitual necktie wearer until the dawn of my teens and the shadow – the self that is less flexible – has to some extent loomed large for considerably longer.

You have probably come across the idea of 'shadow' and the 'shadow self' before. In Jungian psychology it refers to the mainly negative parts of someone's personality that they do not identify with or recognise. Writers use it to evoke the widespread fear of darkness; the fear of monsters lurking there in the shadows ready to pounce and destroy. It becomes synonymous with a place of hiding, concealment and danger. Sometimes those dangers are very, very real; more often however, the fear is illusory or over-stated.

It may be that you do indeed have a shadow of darker proportions, perhaps as a result of abusive relationships or of bullying or of drug abuse. The shadow can be a way of hiding these away from view simply in order to survive.

In the context of this book however, I am using 'shadow' to refer to things cloaked in darkness simply because they have not yet had light shone upon them. They are not the product of deep psychological damage, merely things your psyche has chosen to put to one side and forgotten about, rather like a toy tossed into darkness at the back of a cupboard and then dismissed from conscious thought. But these shadows do still have an impact, however subconsciously. They may, for example, result in avoiding jobs that involve risk or failure. The reason has been lost in the midst of your history, but the impact has remained.

This is one of the reasons for creating and revisiting your Timeline. Sometimes that is all that is needed: bringing these shadowy events into the light of the present is enough to rob them of their negative effects. That is what happened with the realisation about my tie-wearing history; informal dressing is now much more acceptable, and somehow makes being informal amongst friends and acquaintances easier.

By casting light upon the shadows, you are also beginning to reframe or manage your own psychology. You have the opportunity to proactively author a different version of the story; one that robs the power of the shadows. It won't be a work of fiction – or at least no more so than any story from your past – it takes the same facts and events and simply invites you to interpret them or understand them or tell them in a different light. After all, any story is an interpretation of an assortment of incidents, emotions, characters and locations linked so that they combine into a coherent pattern that is called 'the story'. That pattern may be established deliberately and consciously but many are constructed sub-consciously, often as a result of fear or the avoidance of pain or failure. They are never the totality: veiled within the shadows of memory, of past hurts, influences and mistakes, there is always more that could have been added or connected differently. And that might construct a very different story.

As you have been revisiting your Timeline, you may have found that something you have added later has changed the significance of a whole range of associated events and your interpretation of them – rather like my necktie and associated sense of needing to do things 'properly'.

As I grew older, and certainly as I grew into leadership roles, that sense of the 'proper' was useful. Amongst other things it enabled me to behave 'properly' as a leader should, at least according to my understanding. Like many people, I was thrust into my first leadership role totally untrained and unprepared, so I naïvely assumed I would be viewed and treated by my colleagues just as I was before but that I had some additional power of decision-making. But, one of the hardest things to accept was that I was *treated* differently and placed apart, and that's when a shadow from my past emerged and I became rather formal and aloof – I was trying to do things properly.

Of course, this produced very fertile ground for things to fester away in my subconscious, which was where I placed my negativity and worries. I left them there, ignored in the shadow regions. This then fed my insecurities, and since much of this book has been written using the analogy of storytelling, you can image how the plot was simmering away ready to burst out: *there be monsters lurking!* Thankfully, I had a great team and before long, one of them took me to one side, sat me down and in effect coached me into more mature leadership.

In the course of my career since then, I have worked with scores of CEOs and managing directors, and every one of them has said the same thing: nothing prepares you for running your own company! Partly that is because when you don the mantle of CEO those around you suddenly treat you differently. Partly it is the realisation that everyone is now looking to you as the final arbiter and guide. Everyone looks to you to sort out their problems. And everything that goes wrong – well ultimately that's your fault as well: the bad hiring decision, the trickle of wasted money that becomes a torrent, the market that shifts unexpectedly – all your fault. This all contributes to create a shadow. The shadow is partly the loneliness of being at the top and it is fed by the combination of pressure and responsibility. Whatever the reason, you are bound to have experienced times of unprecedented pressure, which is when you are likely to retreat into the shadows. When the spotlight gets too bright and intense, the best place to hide is out of the glare in the shadows. But that is a dangerous place to hide because it is inhabited by the ghosts from your past.

Much better, but infinitely more difficult, is to remain in the glare, and tough it out. It's not easy, but it's what the spiritually-intelligent leader would do. They eschew the shadows and remain in the spotlight.

So, when darkness threatens to envelop, the first task is to check whether it is created by a shadow in your own past. Here's an example of that: I once found the female CEO of a company I worked for particularly difficult, and we would regularly argue and spar until (according to the story I've authored about those events) she would pull rank and tell me to do it her way. Since she held the power, I had to obey; so if I could find any way at all to get out of meetings with her, I would. I cannot say that I behaved particularly well in this situation. Then I had an epiphany. I realised she reminded me of both my mother and an aggressive undermining schoolteacher I once had, and the combination meant I was behaving like the naughty adolescent schoolboy, retreating into the shadows to lick my wounds!

Here was a story I had to both revisit and re-author. It was all too easy to demonise her and exonerate myself. So the new story is to remind myself of the occasions when she did indeed praise me (including a very complimentary testimonial); remembering all the opportunities I had and the many things I learnt during that time and – in particular – remembering the clients whose feedback and thanks gave me great pleasure and pride. I made a difference to a lot of people during that time and I gained a lot of experience and knowledge. It also taught me some lessons about how I behave in those situations and that I'm much more an entrepreneur running my own business than a corporate being. I can finally look back to that time and see the successes as well as being grateful for lessons I probably couldn't have learnt in any other context. I can now see that time in a new light and begin to deal with it in a new way. I am no longer a victim of my circumstances but a learner from them.

There is a powerful 'alchemy of transformation' that can come from revisiting and retelling your story

Following the key theme of this book, the important thing is to proactively consider what story you choose to tell about yourself. And in order to do that you need to know yourself and be able to stand apart from yourself. This is what Ben Horowitz, co-founder of Andreessen Horowitz, calls: managing your own psychology. Know yourself, know what works for you, know how to handle yourself. And then you will begin to see the story emerge. Then check your own rationale: every workaholic can give you a great justification for their behaviour; it doesn't make it any less detrimental.

Where might your story be influenced by a shadow from your past? If there is one, how will you deal with that?

In one of our Case Studies, **Neal Gandhi** is facing a personal crisis, as even the successes of his latest business venture cannot disguise the failure of his marriage. Here we follow Neal as he faces his shadows and sees the light.

Neal Gandhi had a realisation. "The problem was me, so I sat down with a new pad of paper and wrote my name on top, together with this mission: 'You're a new project – work out who you are.'" It took him a year including therapy to become clear about his values, purpose and what he believed in, and then to start to reset his life accordingly. Sometime during this process he asked his mentor, "Is it possible to be nice and make money?" His mentor laughed and remarked that it just needed to be done in the right way.

Another thing that happened during this realignment was meeting an HR Director on a train who had known him 20 years previously. "There was no doubt you'd get there," he'd commented, "but with bodies on the roadside of people you'd squashed along the way."

These two pivotal points – the therapeutic process and this honest assessment of Neal's ruthlessness – helped him to address his shadow side; the darkness that was preventing him from seeing the light.

Then a distant relative asked Neal to help set up a cleaning business. At the time he was reluctant. But something seemed to prompt him into accepting. "And as I did so, I realised the challenges for businesses around paying the living wage and treating employees with respect. I realised that it is possible to pay a living wage, run a business and be profitable for shareholders and stakeholders."

This further clarified his sense of purpose: to build businesses that value their employees, who serve customers well and still generate a return for all stakeholders. But he was also aware of a further dimension that working on his shadow side had uncovered: he had recently come across an organisation called Conscious Capitalism and had been drawn to it because of its core values of building an interdependent culture around shared values that promote business growth and benefit all stakeholders including staff, investors, clients and the wider community. The emphasis is that 'every business has a purpose that includes, but is more than, making money. By focusing on its Higher Purpose, a business inspires, engages and energises its stakeholders.'

For Neal, "it showed me that others were doing the same thing; so I began investing in businesses employing the Higher Purpose principle." He has even walked away from a mega-deal because he was uncomfortable with some of the ethical elements involved.

Does that mean Neal has abandoned everything from his past in favour of this new purpose? No: Neal estimates that in his current Companies Portfolio, about half of his investments pre-date this new alignment, but what he does remark on is that the most enjoyable and satisfying of his companies are the ones governed by the principle of Higher Purpose. "I also suspect that these companies, over a 10-year period, will out-perform the others. They are certainly the ones where it's easier to make decisions." Neal aims to concentrate on, "massively sustainable companies that change the world."

As the Case Studies in this book have shown, sometimes the trigger for change comes from an unexpected and traumatic event: with Neal Gandhi it was the failure of his marriage and an awareness of his ruthless shadow side. Sometimes it comes from a relatively managed and predictable event such as a resignation. Sometimes it is triggered by a memory associated with a photograph, as with my tie. Sometimes it comes from sharing a story from our past with a new person – as with you, perhaps?

Ralph, one of the central characters in Paulo Coelho's novel *Eleven Minutes*, has always been reluctant to share anything about himself with anybody. When his friend Maria presents him with a pen and explains why it is so significant to her, he feels compelled to share something about his past in return. He carefully reaches up onto a bookshelf and retrieves a carriage from a toy train set. He tells her that this carriage was part of his childhood electric train set. He holds it tightly to his chest and says, "When I was a child, I wasn't allowed to play with it on my own because my father said it had been imported from the United States and was very expensive. So I had to wait until he felt like setting up the train in the living room. But he spent most Sundays listening to opera. That's why the train survived my childhood but never gave me any happiness. I've still got the entire track, the engine, the houses, even the manual, because I had a train that wasn't mine and with which I've never played... This pristine train set always reminds me of a part of my childhood that I never lived because it was too precious..."

In the search for a new direction, a new future, it is sometimes necessary to ask whether there are parts of your life to this point that you have never lived and that therefore remain undeveloped. Naturally everyone has countless things they might have done in their lives but did not, usually for very good reasons. But we are referring to things that would have been a *significant* part of healthy development had they been allowed to flourish. For Ralph it was as dramatic as impacting his whole childhood, leaving him insular, protectionist and devoid of a sense of fun. The item he describes, the train set, becomes a symbolic representation of a lost childhood; it is quite likely he would have been visualising a particular story or time when he had asked his father to be allowed to play with the train set and been told his father was 'too busy'. Those stories remain part of the wider life-story but often hidden under layers of life experience.

Shadows that have not been confronted can significantly limit plans for the future

In Ralph's case, by exposing a piece of his lost childhood to his friend Maria – one that had ultimately resulted in him being unable to make any emotional attachments to people or things in case he broke them, and to lack a sense of levity and playfulness – he was able to revisit those experiences and shine a light onto those shadows so that he viewed them literally in a new light. He can't change the actual past but he can begin to share his thoughts and feelings and risk being vulnerable as part of learning to establish deeper relationships: that people might indeed actually have time to spend with him rather than always being "too busy".

This is not about writing a new story denying the shadow; or denying that what created the shadow ever happened. No, it is about recognising the *impact* of the shadow and creating a new story, a new future that is not dominated by the shadow. Shadowsthat have not been confronted can significantly limit plans for the future.

ACTIVITY 7.1 – WHAT'S LOOMING IN THE SHADOWS?
Timeline/Story 9

This is a key Activity and I strongly recommend allowing plenty of time for it, especially if the first reaction to it is that it does not apply to you! It does not have to be completed in one go but do make sure you have blocks of time sufficient to allow you to reflect, think, explore, challenge and simply sit in silence.

One of the important things an author does in order to keep a story interesting and build to the crucial climax is drop some hints along the way both to warn the reader and also to build a sense of tension: why can't that main character see what they're doing and where it will lead? Why can't they spot the juggernaut, literal or symbolic, that's hurtling towards them? It's so obvious... At several points over the past few pages I have been asking you to look back at your past, your story, your timeline, to see where there might be hints about your unfolding life.

+ Now, at this point in your Timeline I am asking you to look for for the juggernauts looming in those shadows that might be coming your way.

+ What might they be? Or, if there are juggernauts that have hit you in the past why did you miss them?

+ What were they and where were the early warnings?

+ If they were concealed in the shadows, what did the shadow represent for you? What lessons were they trying to teach you?

SHADOWS AND JUGGERNAUTS

On one occasion when doing this Activity, I realised that externally imposed sales targets did not motivate me and were in fact counter-productive: at some deep level I expected to fail. After some thought I remembered that my parents, anxious not to spoil me as an only-child, always wanted more from me: whatever I did, it was never good enough. This was a deep shadow for me. What I needed was to be able to set my own goals that motivated me and not to be intimidated by the expectations of others. And what does motivate me is having total responsibility for my targets, objectives, inputs and responsibilities. As an employee, therefore, I'm a liability. As a self-employed businessperson I'm ideally qualified. What really motivates me is change, along with freedom and flexibility. I need to be able to monitor and assess my own performance against the things that matter most to me: especially making a difference to the wellbeing of other people. That gave me a whole different focus for my future. But what I also learned was that money is important to me. Not at the top of the list but certainly high up. When I looked at these revelations, I could see a new future forming.

One of the features of this point in time when the future seems unclear or uncertain is structure or lack of it. If this has been triggered by retirement, even though in a way that is predictable, this lack of structure seems to be even more acutely experienced. The between-projects entrepreneur can feel something similar. Commonly there is the post-event honeymoon period of holiday or travel, buying the yacht, paying off the mortgage, recuperating after the pressure... and then typically one of several things kick in: boredom, guilt, or identity-loss.

Serial entrepreneurs are usually people who get bored quickly and want a new and different challenge. Most CEOs and MDs take busy-ness as second nature and have operated at high energy, high pressure and high adrenalin for so long that when it abruptly ends and there is no pattern, structure or business to replenish it, there can be feelings of guilt at doing 'nothing', or worse, of depression at having nothing to do. And in terms of loss of identity, many have become so used to thinking of themselves as 'the boss'; of being the focus of attention; of describing themselves in terms of what they do, that it becomes difficult to find any self-reference point.

Rationally it makes no sense – you are still the same person – but unfortunately the heart, the spirit if you like, feels differently and fails to listen to the cold logic. It is to do with identity and the status accorded by society to the 'gainfully' employed (whatever that means). That is why the answer lies in the heart (soul) not the head (mind). It seems to me that at various core times in life, at a crossroads or on the edge of a precipice, life offers you the chance to re-assess, to re-examine those things previously taken for granted and, if you find them no longer satisfying, to set off in a new direction.

In order to do that, life offers you the opportunity to reframe how you interpret and tell the stories from your past and use this new understanding in order to create a more satisfying, fulfilling future. This is especially true if you stand on the roughly mid-life precipice between the second and third phases of life and its emphasis on integration and giving back.

THE INTEGRATED LIFE (2)
EMBRACE THE SHADOW

So what exactly is the challenge if you are at this point? What is the way forward? Most other personal development books will tell you to walk out from your shadows and leave them behind. They will implore you to identify past 'juggernauts' and ensure you avoid them in the future.

I take a different line. I invite you to accept them as part of what has made you who you are today. I recommend you examine them to see what you can learn from them and how they might be indicators of doors that need to be closed. And then to choose how you will write that new story as you go forwards. You can only live the Integrated Life if you accept that you have good experiences and bad ones; that you have made good decisions and bad ones and will continue to do so. We all have character flaws. We are less than perfect. But the longer you deny them, the more they are allowed to fester in the shadows of your life, the more they will continue to rear their ugly heads at the most inopportune times. In every great story the hero has feet of clay – even Superman has his Kryptonite.

DIYA'S STORY

Despite his warning on timescales, even Surinda is surprised by how long it is before the next catch-up with Diya. There have been several emails in the meantime but mostly inconsequential: "still thinking", "lots of questions, no answers," – that sort of thing. So he's more than a little surprised at her appearance when she pushes open the coffee shop door: she's lost weight and her eyes are dark-ringed but he also notices that her shoulders are thrown back and there's an aura about her he can only describe as defiance. She glances round the tables then smiles and her face lights up as she spots him. Surinda nods to the woman behind the counter and she commences preparation of the pre-ordered beverages.

"Surinda, you have made my life hell!" (Not the start he normally looks for from his clients.) "Those questions you made me look at... you have no idea." She flings her coat over the back of the chair and flops down wearily. "And thank you for more sleepless nights than pregnancy and a new baby."

He's starting to wonder if he's done the right thing after all. Yet she'd always seemed more than capable of any business challenge. Hadn't she won awards, for goodness sake?

Coffee arrives and they sit in silence. In the interval since coming in she seems to have shrunk and her shoulders sag as she warms her hands on the hot liquid in the mug.

"The last few months, it's been like living in a wilderness. Nothing I've tried has taken me any further forward. Just deeper into uncertainty. One door after another is being closed in my face. My friends think I've lost it big-time – I can see it in their faces. I've even tried going back to doing what I used to do but nothing fits. None of the old things work any more but nothing new does either." She fiddles with the teaspoon, turning it round in the sugar bowl, cutting swathes through the fine brown crystals.

It's a long time since Surinda has found it this difficult to keep quiet and not jump in.

"On the plus side, I have identified several things that I fear happening, apart from the obvious fear of turning into my father!" she joked. "I realised that the moment I stop being the entrepreneur and doing what I've always done, then I'm fearful of being thrown on the scrapheap. After all, being an entrepreneur is all I ever have done. And I fear the loss of challenge, of everything becoming staid and boring. Without all that, who am I? I've nothing to contribute whatsoever."

Again Surinda is tempted to intervene and point out her many achievements beyond business: her children, her relationship with her siblings and their children. But it's still not the right moment.

"It just feels as if there's been a shadow hanging over my mind and it's stopping me seeing how to go forwards. All I can hear is my father telling me that's what happens when you turn your back on your family and that it's exactly what I deserve."

"Tell me more about those shadows and your father's voice."

"Well, it came out of you telling me to write my life story. Whenever I tried to write something down, I couldn't visualise anything. There was just a voice telling me what to write. Then after a few weeks of this it dawned on me the voice was my father's. It was like everything I'd written had been dictated by him. Nothing is in my own voice. But when I went back, when I tried to find stories with my own voice there was just blackness, this shadow. Nothing. That's when I hit the brick wall."

"Okay, Diya, I want you to open up your notebook at your Timeline. Then I want you to pick an entry at random – something from when you were, let's say, in your teens."

"Yes, got that. Leaving home to live in my first flat. Eighteen."

"What did your father's voice tell you about that?"

"That I was throwing my life away. I should be going to university and how much they'd given up so I could get good grades. He refused to speak to me for six months."

"Looking back, what would you have liked to say to him?"

"Ummm... That there are more ways of learning than through studying books. That I would make him proud of me even though I wasn't going to university."

"So in your eyes, was that move and period of time a success or a failure?"

"He never let me forget that he thought I'd let him down."

"But in your voice, Diya. This is your story, not his."

"In mine? I guess it was... a success. It was the first time I ventured out from under the family wing and it showed me I could stand on my own two feet, and that I had the determination to do it."

"Good. Now I want you to go back and do the same with each of the other significant events on your Timeline. And for every one I want you to make sure you do it with your own voice, not your father's. It's harder than it sounds but with practice you'll get there. Then, I want you to look at all the times you were successful and draw a line to connect them and look at what they have in common. Do the same with the times when things weren't going well and see what connects those. Do any patterns arise? When you've done that, call me: I want to hear you tell me the stories and if I think I'm hearing someone else's voice I'll call you on it! OK?"

ACTIVITY 7.2 – ACTIVATE

Plan to ensure you are active in body, mind and spirit. A hike or long walk for example can feed the mind via route-planning and compass-following; the body through exercising the muscles; and the spirit by simply appreciating the beauty and tranquillity of the great outdoors. View this as an opportunity to re-energise and inspire. So, I invite you to plan and execute this walk over the next few days.

Plan four places on the walk where you can stop for a while to reflect on each of the questions below, at successive stops. At each one, spend at least the first thirty seconds simply taking deep breaths in and out; then look at the questions for that Stop.

STOP 1: Simply spend five minutes looking around you. If you're in open countryside or a forest or in a town park or a city street, what range of sounds can you hear? What can you smell?

STOP 2: Discover what is beautiful to you at this point.

STOP 3: Look around to find a stone or a rock or a building or similar that might represent you at this point in time. Why?

STOP 4: If a ghostwriter were authoring your life story what would they be talking to you about at this point?

SUMMARY

In this chapter you have had the opportunity to:

+ Identify shadows, their impact and how they may have clouded the story you tell about your life.

+ Shine the light of later experience into those shadows and then construct a different story to tell about them.

- Consider a Case Study of how they dealt with their shadows.

- With the benefit of exercise, to think deeply about your purpose and 'higher purpose', and the parts of your life you've never lived.

"Never look at the trombones – it only encourages them."

A paraphrase from Richard Strauss
(Composer and Conductor)

CHAPTER 8
FLYING

To start this chapter I want to tell you an allegorical story.

THE CIRCUS AND THE FARMER

Once upon a time, a small remote village was visited by a travelling circus. All the villagers marvelled at the freedom of the performers as they flew through the air, the skills of the jugglers as they hurled and caught skittles, swords and even small children from the audience. They laughed with the clowns and cheered the horse riders. The circus folk thrilled them with their joy, their exuberance, their freedom and their skills. Then they were gone.

A day later a small baby was found abandoned just outside the village. No-one could explain how it had survived. But survive it had. And despite exhaustive enquiries, no-one could find where the circus people had moved on to. It was almost as if they had never existed. Only the memories of the villagers and the presence of the baby said otherwise. And so the child was taken in and cared for by a childless farmer and his wife.

The baby grew, became a toddler and then a child. And the more she grew, the more the villagers began to notice her differences. Her hair was deep black and shiny, quite unlike the blond hair of the others. Her nose was long and pointed, quite unlike the short, flat noses of her companions. And she was tall, thin and athletic, easily out-running and out-wrestling even most of the boys who were much shorter and plumper.

Years later the circus returned. If anyone noticed the physical similarities between the girl and the slim circus athletes, no-one said anything. Even the girl herself seemed unaware. As she gazed and marvelled at their prowess she turned to the farmer beside her. "How graceful they are, how free and how skilled."

"Ah yes," sighed the farmer. "They are beholden to no-one. Their time and their life are their own. They are free to come and go, to travel, to practice and to perform as they please. And all welcome them. They are people of freedom and the theatre. You have to be born to that. You and me, we are people of the land."

And so the girl lived and died in that village, one of the people of the land. Because that is what everyone told her she was.

The chances are you are reading this book because, to a lesser or greater extent, you identify with that girl's challenge. You look back at your life so far and on balance it has been good, maybe even great. You have got material success, a strong curriculum vitae and some outstanding people around you.

But now your life no longer satisfies in the same way as it once did. The challenge is to become the acrobat rather than the farmer (with no disrespect to farmers, this being a metaphorical story). You feel tethered to the ground but called to fly. Yet those around you are offering advice more akin to the farmer's.

This chapter challenges you to identify some key themes that will cut you loose to fly and enable you to fly.

The point is that you cannot face the climax of your story still clothed in the robes of what has gone before. It would be like swinging on the trapeze still wearing the farmer's outdoor clothes and boots.

At one level, that can seem like idealistic claptrap. No one can simply walk away from their past as if it never happened or drop it like an outmoded coat. And it would be a travesty to abandon the hard-earned skills and experience that formed Act 2 of your journey. Acts 1 and 2 provide the preparation and the backdrop for Act 3. But they may also prove inadequate to win Act 3's battle. Act 3 requires something substantively different, a paradigm shift.

You cannot face the climax of your story still clothed in the robes of what has gone before

So for example, it is unlikely that the dreams and aspirations of your childhood will provide the tools for Act 3 because the dreams of childhood served their purpose when we are children. They served the function of teaching us about good and evil, about bravery and sacrifice; they dealt with the transmission of myths and traditions. They were about instilling society's norms and values. As we grow older, we need stories of a different style; and your life story is no longer told in the style of a fairy-tale.

The dreams – the aspirations – you had in your teens to mid-twenties are of more relevance and significance, because they were authored at the time when you were exploring and formulating your own values, drivers and motivators. But even they are likely to be insufficient for flying through Act 3; there is usually a strong sense of idealism about them, but perhaps not rooted in reality. There is the feeling you have the power, the insight and the understanding to make a difference in the world whether through politics, social action, religion or work. Yes, of course it is often idealism: in my teens I was going to be an England Rugby International AND save the world through good deeds at the same time as being an accomplished (amateur) actor! No, their importance lies not in their specifics but in what they reveal about your personality, your traits and your values. So for me, it would seem that I need a sense of being in the limelight, of gaining acceptance, recognition and status whilst being able to make a difference in people's lives. There is also something about my need to be creative or innovative, and of putting myself in other people's shoes.

What about the dreams and aspirations you had when you first stepped into business? What did you want to achieve? What did you think you would be giving to it and getting out of it? What did you feel you would be contributing? These values and aspirations have additional significance because they come from our own creativity, our own drivers and desires and calling at a time when we're gaining more power to actually change and control things.

Maybe you never set out with any great dreams? Many entrepreneurs did not: they simply had a great idea, set something up in the back bedroom or garage and then continued head-down as it grew. Or maybe you entered a business because a parent or relative opened an opportunity or maybe owned the company, and then you found it fitted your skills and you rose up the ranks.

That is why, as you stand on the precipice of the Third Act those traits and behaviours give a valuable steer about what will constitute your fulfilled life going forward, so that you can fly rather than be tethered to the ground by outgrown limitations. You are on the precipice of something new and exciting. It may not feel like it, but you are. This is truly the realm of the Hero and many falter at this point, turning back because the chasm in front seems too deep or wide or scary or uncertain. Flying is frightening because the potential to crash is never far away and it takes a paradigm shift in one's Story to be able to take flight.

One of the major fears, often the deal-breaker for those who turn back, is the realisation that you cannot create an inspiring future by simply repeating the past. It really does have to be a new beginning. Some cherished parts of your past now need to be discarded – along with some you will no doubt be all too glad to drop. And attempting any form of bargaining ('If I can just keep this, then I'll happily give up that…') tends to be counter-productive, like going to buy new business clothes but insisting that the tailor include a few pieces from the old garments in the new! Or, perhaps more aptly, bolting a few rusty old aircraft parts onto a new plane.

That future you are aspiring to probably seems a long way off, across a chasm in a promised land that remains illusively indistinct and that has still to be defined and claimed. But it is there. As Jim Preston is about to find out…

As darkness falls, Jim Preston is enjoying chatting over a candle-lit supper with Sue. It's one of the few opportunities they get to be alone together and talk: "… and actually I do genuinely feel as if I'm standing on the edge of something really big. I don't know what it is yet. But I know it's there. I know I'm being called to do it. Good grief, I never thought I'd hear myself saying that!"

"So if you had no constraints, if you could fly free, what would you do, Jim?"

"You know what, in some senses not a lot different to now. What Chris got me to do was look back at when I've been at my best, and I saw that it was when I was given the chance to be creative and to find news ways of doing things. And that's what I've lost in recent years. Too often it was the fear of being left behind that made me cautious and play safe. It was as if I wouldn't exist if I didn't have a job title of some sort – preferably 'Senior'. So when he asked me what my vision was for the next ten years, I really struggled at first. It was only when he helped me look again at my core values that it began to make some sense.

"When I was young I thought I was going to change the world. Now I'm older, I've got a bit more realistic, a bit more pragmatic. So actually, in my next stage of life I just want to leave things better than I found them – not for the whole world but for just a few people. Simple as that, really. I really feel drawn to something around that, it's just that I'm not sure quite what yet. But there's something out there that already excites me."

"Well, maybe you've just got to jump out into the unknown and see where it takes you!"

"And what if..."

"Jim, after all these years haven't you realised yet that life will always be full of 'what ifs...'" She puts an affectionate, slightly despairing, hand on his arm. *"What matters is how you deal with it. After all, what's the worst that could happen?"*

"True. Now where's my laptop – let's see who I can talk to..."

"No! Hang on a minute. I thought this was supposed to be about letting go of the past and flying free! Come on, Jim, if you could do whatever you wanted, if there really weren't any constraints, what would you do?"

"Actually that's harder than it sounds! There's too much choice."

"Come on, Jim. Concentrate. What have you learnt from all these months of navel-gazing?"

"It's not been..." Then he catches the twinkle in her eyes. *"OK, I take your point. What stands out is: It needs to be a new start. Recruiters are only interested in me if I want to do more of the exact same thing as I've been doing for years: that's just past experience not future development. And even then, my age is starting to go against me.*

But I've been at my best when I'm being creative and when I feel I'm making a difference. And actually, that's interesting because, do you remember when I was considering that CEO job, and the guy I met who was looking for investment possibilities? Well, I've got an idea that might well interest him. I might just give him a call now..."

THE EXISTENTIAL LEAP

In storytelling, Acts 1 and 2 generally flow together. There is some Inciting Incident that triggers everything else that follows but the attempts at resolution follow the patterns that have always worked well previously. In 'life' terms they represent the phase where we are concerned with separating ourselves out from our peers and carving out a particular niche that is distinctive. It is about competition and hence can be referred to as the Warrior phase. Getting stuck-in, sleeves rolled up. The classic vocabulary is about 'I' or 'me'.

Act 3 represents a different phase characterised by the recognition that individuals are interconnected and are part of a whole. The emphasis shifts from separating out into joining together, to interconnectedness. It is about giving back, contributing out of experience and knowledge rather than physical strength or hands-on involvement. Hence it is the phase of Wisdom – though its inhabitants may only be in their mid-or late thirties onwards. The classic vocabulary is about 'We' and 'Us'.

What sort of person do you want to be, going forward?

Act 3 lies across the precipice, on the other side of the chasm that must be crossed if your legacy is to be fulfilled. The chasm is both wide and deep. The edge of the abyss is helpfully marked with a warning, a challenge: 'What sort of person do you want to be, going forward?' That is the final hurdle the Hero must overcome. It is the pull of gravity that the aeroplane must defeat if it is to leave the ground and fly. The only way onward is by answering that question. Not all have the courage to even attempt it, especially since abandoning previously accepted paradigms offers no guarantee that there will be a safe landing with new ones.

This is not a crossroads in your life; it is more stark and challenging than that. You have arrived at a 'precipice'. The old land has trailed away from under your feet; the promised land lies across the chasm, tantalising, beckoning and frustratingly out of reach!

If this rings true with your experience, if you are at this point, here comes the critical moment of decision: whether to engage in the final action and leap, or turn away. In writing, this dilemma is called 'the climax'. Interestingly the climax is not the end of the story; the climax is merely the final confrontation that the Hero must overcome. The remainder of the story consists of the Hero's return and the sharing of the spoils, their legacy. But now the character and core values of the Hero have been established in Act 3, there is also the new beginning.

So how do you work out a new direction when all these old assumptions, beliefs, values, motivators no longer seem quite as adequate, satisfying or motivational?

PREPARING TO FLY

At this stage, a degree of preparation is necessary. Without it, without a certain amount of trimming out and casting off, the weight of the past is likely to catapult us into the chasm rather than fly us across into the Promised Land. Here is a salutary tale:

THE BOY AND THE CLOTH BAG

A small boy had a prized possession – a large cloth bag. Everywhere he went he carried it with him. Every time his parents or someone else said something that made him cry or stung him, he drew the sting out from his heart and dropped it into his bag. Every action that he associated with pain, everything he wanted to ward off, was deflected into it. Once in the bag it protected him from hearing or feeling those harsh words and unkind actions again. And he added to it those desires from his own thoughts and heart that others criticised or discouraged, those bits of himself that didn't fit the mould others were expecting him to fill.

Over the years as the boy grew bigger so did the bag. More and more went into it. But the boy didn't seem to notice. After all, it grew as he grew and just became part of his life. And carrying it meant that he was able to become the person that others wanted to see. He grew with their approvals and their expectations; and he put behind him all those things that earned their disapproval.

The boy grew into a youth and for a while the bag seemed sealed. Nothing went into it. In fact he took great pride in the fact that the bag was sealed and that he was now the person he wanted to be.

Life progressed. He got his first career opportunity. He married. He looked at his life as it stretched ahead of him. And he felt contented. Once or twice he was even tempted to leave the bag behind. But whenever he did, he missed its familiarity, he felt incomplete. So he would pick it up again, reasoning, "I'm my own person. I'm not deflecting things into it any more. There's no harm in carrying it with me." And he heaved it back onto his shoulder.

One day, about the time of his thirtieth birthday, his own baby was born – a son. It was as he looked into the still-unseeing eyes of the newborn, as he considered what he wanted for his own son, that once more he became aware of the weight of the sack he carried.

But this time he really was aware of the weight, the enormity of it. And as he became aware of its enormity he also knew as a blinding certainty that he did not want his own son to carry such a burden. He wanted only the best for him. Henceforth this would be his top priority, his greatest commitment. At that same moment, unseen, a tiny bag appeared behind the infant's back...

One of the challenges of preparing to fly is to recognise past expectations that have been placed upon us and that have kept us tethered to the ground, and to begin untying them; removing the debris and detritus within and reducing the weight of the bag.

ACTIVITY 8.1 – FLEXING YOUR WINGS

What will you be when you really do fly? This Activity allows you to get a better sense of your destination, your legacy. I would like you to build on the idea of 'story' as a vehicle to inspire, energise and guide you to fly. So, I want you to take your skills, experience and wisdom – all that you've learned from the Activities you've undertaken in this book up to now – and use these insights to build your (metaphorical) wings, that will enable the paradigm shift, the existential leap across the chasm. The components are already there. All you need to do is assemble them and have the courage to launch yourself.

Might you crash? Yes. Might you get blown off course? Yes. And, picking up an image from an earlier chapter, might there be monsters in the shadows? Yes. But you know from all the work you have done up to this point that this is just fear talking – fear of the change you are about to make.

So, now I would like you to write that story, the one where you flex those wings and fly into the future.

+ Where are you headed and why?

+ What do you need to do to get there?

+ What hurdles might you have to overcome?

+ How will you remove those barriers?

+ What is the ultimate resolution you are aiming for?

As with all the stories you've written as you've worked through this book, reflect on your Timeline and look for clues. Seeds of possibility will have been strewn across your path throughout the course of your life, so look for the green shoots of potentiality to guide your way.

A note of caution must be sounded here. In the archetypal Heroic Myth stories, there will be obstacles in your path that may well take the Hero – you – close to exhaustion, despair and defeat. But never fear: the greatest challenges and obstacles to overcome, the greatest threats to success often precede the denouement – like the coldest part of the night is always just before dawn. This is the point where you are now. This is the moment in the film or book where all seems lost and the Hero must surely fail. But a 'superhuman' or Herculean effort, the ultimate in courage, enables the Hero to fly and claim the ultimate spoils – the legacy. Are you ready for one last push?

Of course, life isn't a Hollywood script, but do not underestimate those final hurdles: they are the equivalent of the last gruelling leg before the marathon's finishing line. Crossing the finishing line – or in our case, leaping the chasm to the Promised Land – requires effort, commitment, focus and resources at the very time these are at their most depleted. They are the times when the shadows of past doubts, failures and insecurities are at their most threatening and the vision for the future can be at its dimmest.

However, the good news about Act 3, once you've made that leap of faith, is that there, you can build the satisfying conclusion of your story, and since that to which you are being called is precisely that – a calling – and because you are now concentrating on those things that give you energy rather than drain it, the resources are there, for the resolution you are dreaming of.

The key is to keep looking ahead. If 'legacy' is important to you, keep focussed on what achieving that will feel like. If it's 'making a difference', keep focused on what that will mean and feel like.

CREATING LEGACY AND MAKING A DIFFERENCE

What is Legacy? Winston Churchill summed this up rather neatly:

"We make a living by what we get, we make a life by what we give."

Legacy is what we give back in Act 3. It is what we choose to leave as our message to the world. It is my aim that by the end of this chapter you will have a clear Action Plan that will guide you towards your Legacy. It will be realistic, focused and energising. It is about how you might move from 'making a living' to 'making a life'. You have already flexed your wings. You are nearly ready to fly.

Indeed, to extend the metaphor one step further, this Action Plan is rather like a flight plan: it focuses on the destination and details the route for getting there. The destination itself is interesting though. Because it is a place of Legacy (of giving back) it is characterised by self-actualisation and self-transcendence, and a sense of the numinous or spiritual; it is a place where you will feel more of a drive to put things back rather than take things out. There is a move to understand who you are in relation to other people – your links and connectivity with them rather than what separates you from them. It is a place of Resolution that will enable you to identify the great gift only you possess in order to make a difference.

Typically, this stage of Wisdom bears little relation to your chronological age but is indicated by a growing awareness of the needs and aspirations beyond your own direct self-interest and that of your family. There is a new sense of being part of something greater. Some, but by no means all, talk of feeling 'called' by something outside of themselves; drawn by something greater that they may refer to as Higher Power.

This is most definitely not a stage of dreaming; it is a stage of action. Many people talk of it as being something they cannot *avoid* doing. Their calling inspires them and generates extraordinary energy and commitment to achieving it – sometimes far more so than in the earlier stage of the Warrior because, this time, fundamentally the calling is values-driven. It is the search for the *transcendent* meaning of work, the things that the psychologist Frederick Herzberg terms satisfaction-building; or that Maslow terms *self-actualisation*. (See Appendix.)

The more you inhabit the third phase of your life where Act 3 takes place, the more you are likely to see and understand connectivity with others and to feel integrated into it.

LEGACY – THE TRUE JOY IN LIFE

We have been looking at what your Legacy might be. Does it have to be world-shatteringly impactful or newsworthy? Certainly not. George Bernard Shaw summed it up wonderfully:

This is the true joy in life, the being used for a purpose recognised by yourself as a mighty one; the being a force of nature instead of a feverish selfish clod of ailments and grievances complaining that the world will not devote itself to making you happy. I am of the opinion that my life belongs to the whole community and as long as I live it is my privilege to do for it whatever I can. I want to be thoroughly used up when I die, for the harder I work, the more I live. I rejoice in life for its own sake. Life is no 'brief candle' to me. It is sort of a splendid torch that I have a hold of for the moment, and I want to make it burn as brightly as possible before handing it over to future generations.

(Epistle Dedicatory, Man & Superman, 1903)

Your legacy is the 'true joy in life', the knowing that you have given your all and that it has made a difference; that you have used and developed to its full the gift uniquely entrusted to you, and that it has made the world a better place for at least some people you have encountered and influenced. It is satisfaction at a job well done – where 'job' means the life you've led rather than narrowly just the work you were paid to do. That is the 'mighty purpose' you and you alone are called to do. And that no one else could do in quite the same way.

It is sacrificial in the sense of being focused on others rather than totally on yourself.

> # Are you a force of nature or a feverish selfish clod of ailments and grievances complaining that the world will not devote itself to making you happy?

So let's move on to identify what this legacy of yours might be. You now have at least some idea of where you are at your best, what matters most to you and at least an inkling if not a full-blown vision of where you want to be heading – the Flexing Your Wings Activity 8.1 detailed much of this so look on it as being the preliminary sketch for a painting; the template for the denouement.

AVOIDING DISTRACTIONS, DIVERSIONS AND DEAD ENDS

Finding the way forward can take a long time. The right way may not yet be opening in front of you but it is very likely that wrong ways are closing behind you. In times of prolonged uncertainty, the temptation is to turn back to what you have previously done or to over-rely on the skills, experiences and habits of the past so that they limit rather than set free the future. Then you are likely to continue what Palmer calls, 'a work that is not mine to do,' even if that work is laudable, necessary, noble and meeting a real human need.

Some years ago I was heavily involved in local radio as a volunteer presenter and producer at a hospital. I loved it. And when I reached the point where I wanted a new challenge in work it seemed like the obvious career door to push. I discovered that the local radio station where I grew up and had lived for twenty years was indeed looking for a professional presenter in two specialisms where I had considerable personal experience. They assured me they would welcome an application and in fact, "I was exactly what they were looking for". My application went in a matter of hours later. And there the opportunity halted. I heard nothing. No interview. Nothing. Door firmly closed. A few months later a totally different opportunity opened up in front of me – one that has been a significant part of my life ever since.

You may be thinking that all I am doing here is putting a later justification on something where I simply was not good enough. That it was perhaps a matter of better people applying, and of course you may be right. But in light of what later emerged it makes more sense to me, it feels more accurate, to recognise that my unique gift and contribution was not in that direction and that I was being called and pulled in a different direction.

When doors are closed to us, especially if in a public way, it can be both embarrassing and discouraging. Even more so if nothing else seems to emerge straight away. So it is fair to ask, 'Is it possible to be forewarned? Can you spot in advance where a proffered opportunity might be a diversion from what you are being called to do?' Is it possible to avoid flying off to a completely un-satisfying destination? The answer is yes. The better you know yourself, your deepest core values, your vision and your unique gift, the more likely you are to focus your vision and its implementation in the direction to which you are being called.

In the Case Study below, Mike Johnson describes some of the attributes that he believes enable us to avoid dead ends and disasters.

CASE STUDY
The case for courage

Mike thinks that in order to develop your gift, you must have the courage to believe in what you are doing. Believing in what you are doing is interesting. At one level it can simply mean working hard and doing your best, but at a deeper level it is about having a vision and the courage to know where you are going with it. Consequently, this is where your gift or legacy evolves. Having vision gives you a longer-term perspective; it enables you to harness your energy and drive towards your gift. When you have identified what it is you are being called to do in this next phase of life, you will have a great belief in what you are doing and you will know you are doing it for the right reasons, but you still need the courage to fulfill the vision.

Courage is a key attribute of many great leaders whose legacies are undeniably world-changing: Churchill was no angel but he had both charisma and vision and the courage of his convictions. Courage is a key attribute of Nelson Mandela because he made such a difference for good despite the way in which he himself had been treated: he had the courage to speak out for what he believed to be right as part of his vision for the Rainbow Nation. And thirdly, Gandhi, for what he was able to achieve against the odds through nonviolent direct action, which takes perhaps the most courage of all. Whilst we cannot all leave such incredible legacies, Mike believes that courage is a key quality in achieving your calling.

I asked Mike what changes he would like to see in the workplace that would allow a more natural emergence of Legacy.

"I would like to see a cultural shift in our values such that the 'giving back' phase of life is credited with as much importance as our education and career. So many people crash and burn at the end of a successful working life – because what is there of value in the next phase? Retirement and a life of golf or gardening fill most people with fear. There is little preparation for the end of one's working life and so there is no vision for what comes next. That's why it's so important to be clear and courageous about your legacy, so that your focus can shift without a fall into the chasm of depression or entropy."

In another Case Study, Andrew Stone, describes this third phase – Act 3 – as becoming Selfless:

"There's been a gradual realisation that we're not separate independent beings but that we are interconnected on every level: what we do to the earth and all beings, we do to ourselves. So there is a growing need to become selfless and consider what's good for all. If it's in business then that means the staff, Board, shareholders and wider community/ecology. In Act 3 of our lives, that means looking outwards towards the common good of humanity whether that's on a micro or macro scale. To help me with that understanding, I now meditate for 40 minutes at 4am every day 'in order to step outside my ego.' It is also about developing a different part of the brain."

Selflessness affects our outlook and therefore our behaviours. For example we are likely to become more focused on helping the personal development of other people, both for their contribution to the business and for their own growth. Andrew tells the story of a man he once met who worked at Marks & Spencer's. This man desperately wanted to leave to fulfil his calling to become a Buddhist monk. He spoke to his line manager, telling him how much he supported the company values and had enjoyed working there, but that he felt the need to follow his inner calling. His line manager said, 'There may come a point in the coming months when you'll begin to wonder if you did the right thing. I want you to know there'll be a job open for you for the next 9 months should you need it.' The man said, 'If it hadn't been for the willingness of my line manager to support my personal growth with the reassurance of a job should anything go wrong, I don't know if I would've had the courage to fulfil my dream." In Andy's opinion, the M&S line manager, was acting with a Selflessness that marks him out as someone acting from a place of Legacy within Act 3 of his life."

ACTIVITY 8.2 – FREE RANGE THINKING

This Activity simply consists of a number of unrelated questions. Like the proverbial examination, attempt all questions – but this time, feel free to spend as much time as you want on each one. This builds on the Flexing your Wings exercise and is laying the groundwork for your Action Plan.

+ What is beautiful to you?

+ If you could do just one outstanding thing next and you were guaranteed not to fail — what would you do?

+ What's stopping you?

+ What has 'brought you up short' or caught you completely unawares and left you speechless – and why?

+ When are you happy?

+ When have you felt drawn or compelled into a particular course of action by a greater calling? What was the story?

+ What is your biggest fear or threat at this time?

+ If you had to describe your mission in life, what would it be?

+ Who would you describe as today's spiritual leaders? Why?

+ What do you yearn for most, deep down in your soul?

INVESTING WISELY: TIME V ENERGY

As your vision for the phase of Wisdom becomes clearer and more detail appears for what that might mean for you, it enables you to use your time more wisely. Those things peripheral to what is emerging can be discarded. There are fewer 'blind alleys' or dead-end roads to pursue. There are fewer distractions. You are less likely to apply for any job that comes up or accept any interview or chase companies that you are never realistically going to connect with on a deeper level. What this means is you begin to invest more not just in fewer things (that is simply good Time Management) but also in those things closest to your vocation. A recent article (*Harvard Business Review* 24) makes a helpful distinction between 'time' and 'energy' arguing that you put energy into things that you feel passionate about and that are important to you. On the rest you simply spend time. And, they conclude, while 'time' spent is gone, 'energy' spent is renewable and helps build physical, mental AND *spiritual* energy (Italics mine).

'Time' spent is gone, 'energy' spent is renewable

It therefore makes sense to make sure you concentrate on those things that are energy generators. The soul (the 'location' of the spirit) is like the nuclear reactor's core, the generator of effective energy. Energy is generated and renewed by 'sweet spot' activities (what I previously referred to as Signature Strengths) – those things you would probably describe as absorbing, fascinating and engrossing. These activities generate energy, passion and spirit and are food for the soul. They are important signposts signalling the direction of our calling.

THE LAUNCH PAD

I would now like you to bring together in one place all that you have learnt about your vision, your values, your strengths, the things you need to have and the things you need to avoid in order to achieve your Legacy. You are going to do that once again by telling a story.

ACTIVITY 8.3 – FAST FORWARD

+ Imagine your life 5 years from now, where you have successfully drawn your skills, values and vision together to create your Legacy.

+ Write down the exact day, month and year.

+ Next, imagine that today is the day that you have finally achieved your vision. Using the present tense describe how your vision has fallen into place. What have you achieved? Feel the excitement and satisfaction.

+ Look around: what are you actually doing? Enjoy the sensations and accolades. Describe how you feel and what this success enables you to do.

I'd really like to read your story's climax: what you see opening up before you and your vision of Legacy. So please email your story to me: **peter@TheSpiritedLeader.com**.

Which leads me on to the final Act 3 denouements for Jim and Diya.

DIYA MANDAL – EPILOGUE

One of the things Diya has now learnt is that she does her best thinking outdoors, walking. Whether that is because her father's voice still echoes around her home and work, she is not sure. But it doesn't matter. These walks have become precious times of reflection, of learning to recognise her own voice and then actually listening to it. But the open spaces, the fresh air and the sounds of the city just seem to be a place where she gets a sense of calling.

She's writing the current stage of her Timeline and reflecting on the transformational eighteen months. Sometimes the fresh understanding had come through a tortuous and painful re-examination of a past event (such as finding that in every one she was being compared unfavourably with her older brother); sometimes it was an unconnected insight (such as realising just how influential her guilt at being successful and earning a lot of money affected her outlook). Sometimes it led her down a dead-end such as actually applying for jobs with charities only to find herself thoroughly disheartened at their lack of creative entrepreneurial thinking so that she had to rapidly backtrack. But slowly, clarity began to emerge out of the blackness and shadows. As time went on, those dead-ends and diversions became less and less frequent.

Later, when she restarted her cherished professional speaking once more, she described it as being like a sculptor chiselling away tiny splinters of stone, one at a time, to reveal a nugget of wisdom; she read somewhere that Michelangelo had talked about creating his masterpiece by simply chipping away all the bits of stone that weren't David. She empathised.

So now, she has her future sculpted: because she has identified the things to which she has felt called. Each in its own way continues to challenge and build her business skills. And each allows her to give something back. Her Foundation allows her to seed fund start-up businesses that themselves want to make a difference, providing they are run as commercially-viable enterprises. The professional speaking has opened up platforms across the world because she has the credibility of having delivered the goods and it allows her to talk about her own evolving story in a way that inspires and guides others to do the same.

And, most surprising of all, at least to Surinda, she is indeed running the family business, albeit as Chair while mentoring her brother Pranav and sister Vani as joint Managing Directors. After much soul-searching, Diya realised that in taking the reins of her father's business, she could at long last, still his constant voice in her head. She was more like him than she wanted to admit, and in running the business, she could finally release any remnants of guilt about not being a good enough daughter, but in her own way, and on her own terms.

All these elements combined allow her, as she often says from the platform, the ideal opportunity to fulfil her calling and use her skills for a better world, at least in some small measure. And it's every bit as challenging, stressful and demanding as buying and selling companies. But infinitely more rewarding because it's what she feels called to do.

JIM PRESTON – EPILOGUE

Twelve months on and Jim Preston looks a different person. He's relaxed and sun-tanned, his back is ramrod straight and his shoulders are pushed back to face the world. This time his Jaguar car pulls into a car park behind a single story brick building sporting the sign Preston Medical Engineering below which is printed JIM PRESTON, CEO. He pauses for a moment before getting out, running through the day's agenda in his mind and getting ready to enter the fray. It may be a start-up but already the order books are more than healthy. He smiles with his daily reminder of how, the moment he'd met the investor and the entrepreneur, he just knew he was coming home, as if it had been meant to be. Not just the people but also the product: the opportunity to develop cheap, lightweight, dust-proof, miniature casings that would protect medical equipment in remote parts of the developing world. Truly something to be proud of.

As he climbs out of the car, a rugby ball bounces out and he picks it up before tossing back on top of numerous kitbags that almost fill the car's interior. Each is marked 'Kettlebrough Rugby Club Under 18s' and in smaller letters, 'Sponsored by Preston Medical Engineering'. Being the Club's kitman might not be the most obvious role for their new sponsor but he likes it: it gives him a chance to chat to the youngsters, gee them up, without any of the other responsibilities. "A bit like the team uncle," he thinks – blissfully unaware that his team nickname is actually 'Granddad'.

So you now approach the last Activity in the book, when all the components finally fit together like the pieces of a jigsaw and you feel that you have finally encapsulated the vision that will enable you to make a difference in the world using your gifts, talents and experience to the full – and beyond. Ultimately all the energy you need in order to fly comes from aligning your vision with your deepest values. This gives you the hope and strength to take delivery of your gift. Now, you can fly.

ACTIVITY 8.4 – TOWARDS LEGACY: YOUR ACTION PLAN

Spend some time re-reading and re-imagining what you wrote in the previous Activity 8.3.

- Once again, project yourself forward to the successful end of the next five years. Once you feel fully immersed in the success, look back: what are the three crucial steps you need to put in place in order to get from where you are now to where you are five years from today?

- What barriers do you have to overcome?

- Take each of the three steps and break them down into Goals for each of the intervening five years.

- Then starting from today, add in the key Action Steps that will ensure you achieve your Goals.

- How will you know when you have achieved each of them and how will you celebrate them?

Who will you share this with so that they can encourage and challenge you? Remember that those closest to you may not be the best companions because subconsciously they may not actually want you to change if it has an impact on them. A coach is ideal; it needs to be someone wise, who you trust and with whom you can be completely honest – as they will be in return.

WHY NOT?

Although I have used this quote previously, I want to end with it too, because it is so inspirational, it bears repeating:

> "Some men see things as they are and say 'Why?' I dream of things that never were and say, 'Why not?'"

Why not?

For further information and to discuss support and coaching contact Peter Hyson via The Spirited Leader website:
www.peterhyson.com

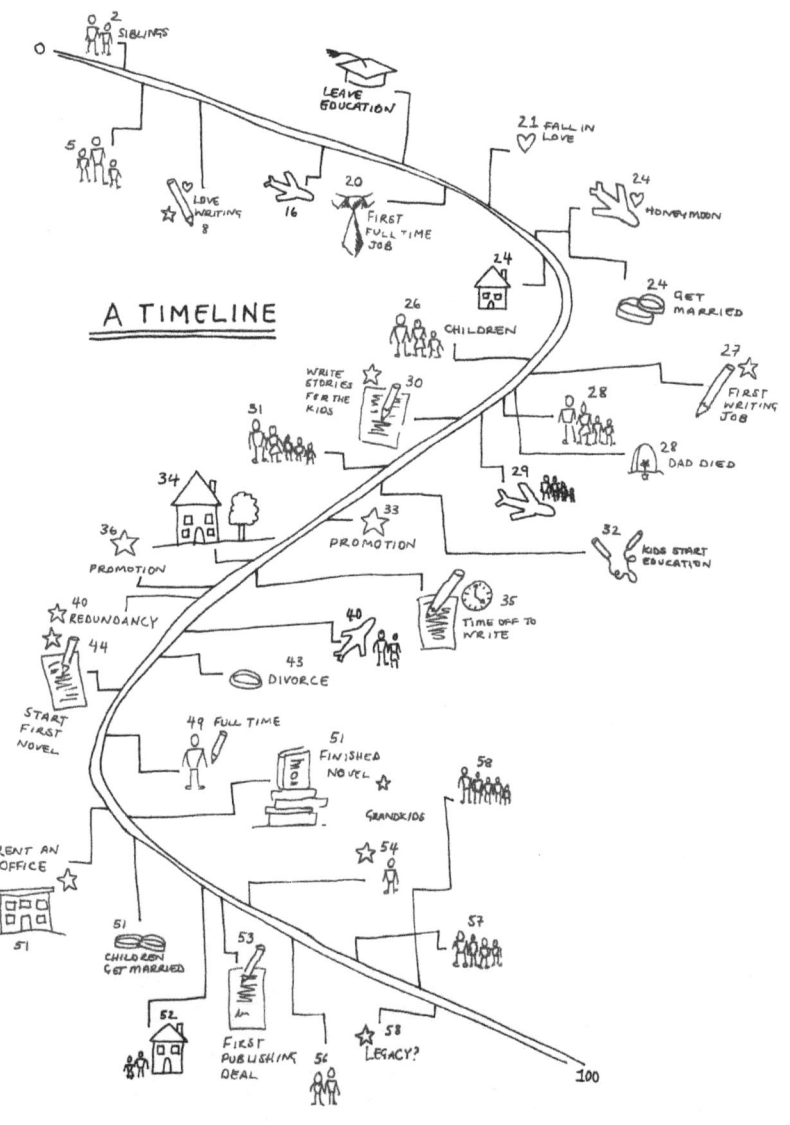

An example of a Timeline

APPENDIX

This chapter provides some additional depth for some of the topics covered elsewhere in the book.

Chapter 3
Maslow's updated Hierarchy of Needs

Hertzberg

self-transcenders*

Builds satisfaction

self-actualisation

self-esteem

- - - - - - - - - - - -

Reduces dissatisfaction

social belonging

safety and security

basic survival

* Maslow found that the healthiest, most developed adults were not the 'self-actualisers' he identified earlier in his career – but the 'self-transcenders': those who moved beyond ego into service to others and the whole of society. (*The Farther Reaches of Human Nature*)

(Maslow's Hierarchy appears in many different forms in many different publications.)

CHAPTER 4
Gateway Terminology

I have used this term in several chapters in the book. A gateway is something that not only marks the transition from one place to another, it also allows you a view from one place into the next. Gateway Terms therefore are words used by yourself or someone else that shine a light or reveal a glimpse into another place. If you hear yourself talking about legacy or inspiration or purpose in life, or about wisdom or being drawn to do something, these are Gateway Terms. What deeper insight or meaning or search are they highlighting?

Typical (but by no means comprehensive) Gateway Terminology

Accountable
Achievement
Advancement
Adventure
Affection
Alchemy
Belonging
Calling
Clarity
Collaboration
Commitment
Community

Competitiveness
Co-operation
Creativity
Destiny
Diversity
Economic security
Ethical
Fame
Family happiness
Flexibility
Freedom
Friendship
Fulfilment
Gift
Give back
Greater good
Health
Helpfulness
Honesty
Humanity
Inner harmony
Innovation
Inspire/ation
Integrity
Intuition
Involvement
Legacy
Loyalty
Making a difference
Meaning
Mission
Openness
Personal development
Pleasure
Power
Presence

Purpose
Quality
Recognition
Respect for individuals
Respect for self
Responsibility
Security
Self
Sharing
Soul
Spirit/uality
Support
Teamwork
Trust
Vision
Vocation
Wealth
Wisdom

But **especially** for this context it might include:

Give back
Something missing
Fulfilment
Legacy
Purpose/Higher Purpose
Meaning
Is this all there is?
Soul
Mission
Vocation
Calling

The quote that so startles Diya is from TS Eliot's poem *The Journey of the Magi* and sourced from *Collected Poems 1909-1962.*

CHAPTER 5

Elisabeth Kübler-Ross and stages of bereavement

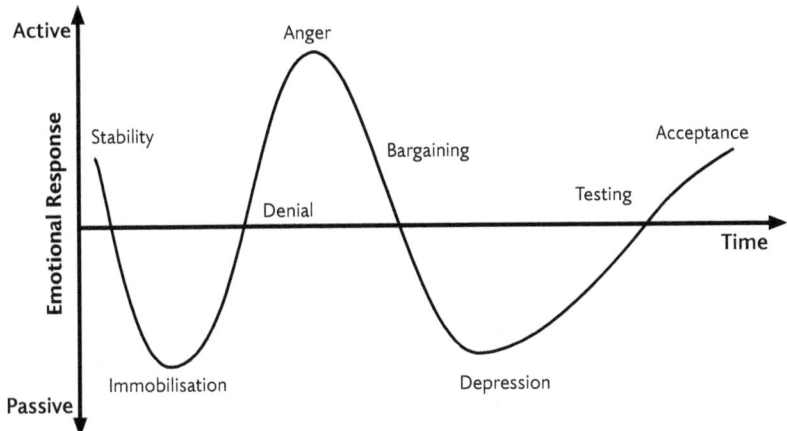

Adapted from the Kübler-Ross Bereavement Cycle

IMMOBILISATION: the shock of the bereavement, even if expected, produces inertia, a kind of frozen state before the pain sets in. This is often true when bad news is given, for example an illness diagnosis or a redundancy. Nothing can be taken in.

DENIAL: typically just what it says: it can't be real, this can't be happening to me.

ANGER: it's not fair; I/they don't deserve this; I'm going to fight back. How can the world possibly be carrying on as if nothing has happened? Or it can be anger with the self for not being there, not having done more or not seeing it coming.

BARGAINING: in bereavement it is often with God or a Higher Power: if you do this then I'll do that. In a relationship-break up it might be, can we still be friends?

DEPRESSION: everything just seems too much effort; things can never be the same again.

TESTING: is this a possible new start? Will it last? Have the previous stages really passed?

ACCEPTANCE of the new state

It is rare for anyone to go through all of these stages and in this sequence. It is more common for someone to spend longer in some stages than others and by no means uncommon for someone to flip back into an earlier stage especially in the two phases *below* the line.

CHAPTER 6

Spirituality "*lifts us beyond ourselves and our narrow self-interests,*" notes Jay Conger in his book, *Spirit at Work: Discovering The Spirituality in Leadership* (page 17). It helps us to see our deeper connections to one another and to the world beyond ourselves and there is growing research evidence of how important SQ (Spiritual Intelligence) is as a defining trait for outstanding leadership. In seminars, workshops and keynote addresses I often ask audiences to think about who they admire as outstanding leaders – exceptional ones who might be alive or dead, even fictional – and then to consider what characteristics and behaviours make them so. Many of those defining characteristics on the list can be considered 'spiritual'.

The Characteristics Of Spiritually Intelligent Leaders

Widely-recognised outstanding leaders exhibit traits such as courage; honesty; inspiration; wisdom; humility; generosity; persistence; forgiveness; love; kindness; peacefulness; faithfulness; calmness or equanimity; passion; and vision. They see gifts in others and commit to developing them.

I am convinced they are the most effective means for making a difference and creating a legacy. And, according to researcher Cindy Wigglesworth, they can be both learned and developed.

The 21 Attributes of Spiritually Intelligent Leaders

This is based on the work of Cindy Wigglesworth – see Bibliography.

Ego Self-Awareness
1   Awareness of own worldview
2   Awareness of life purpose (mission)
3   Awareness of values hierarchy
4   Complexity of inner thought
5   Awareness of Ego Self/Higher Self

Universal Awareness
6   Awareness of interconnectedness of all life
7   Awareness of worldview of others
8   Breadth of time/space perception
9   Awareness of limitations/power of human perception
10   Awareness of spiritual laws
11   Experience of transcendent oneness

Ego Self Mastery
12   Commitment to spiritual growth
13   Keeping Higher Self in charge
14   Living your purpose and values
15   Sustaining your faith/spirituality
16   Seeking guidance from Spirit

Spiritual Mastery
17   A wise and effective spiritual teacher/mentor
18   A wise and effective change agent
19   Takes compassionate and wise decisions
20   A calming, healing presence
21   Being aligned with the ebb and flow of life

Any of these might be present in any type of leader; it is their combination and their context that produce the spiritually-aware leader. This spiritually-aware leader is also not afraid to deliver the hard messages and to wash feet as well as set boundaries.

THE BUSINESS BENEFITS OF SQ

While the contribution that Spiritual Intelligence plays in developing outstanding leaders is clear, persuading them and their businesses to seriously invest in it is a different matter. Benefits must be clear not only for personal leadership but also in improving the business bottom line. In this section I start with several quotations about the growing awareness and importance of this in creating a sustainable legacy and in making a difference in the business itself.

"Spirituality positively affects employee and organisational performance by enhancing intuitive abilities and individual capacity for innovation, as well as increasing personal growth, employee commitment and responsibility." (Neck & Milliman: Thought self-leadership: finding spiritual fulfilment in organizational life" *Journal of Managerial Psychology*, 9 (6) 1994.)

"I do believe strongly in leading in a spiritual way. It keeps you from doing many short-term tactical actions that are often wrong for the business and the people. It also gives you immense courage to stand tall against politics." (Janiece Webb, Motorola, 2004 quoted by William Miller in an online article.)

And more specifically...

"... you have to take the whole individual into account. The workaholic is to be avoided because their drive does not generally inspire a team. It can actually be abusive. Those who are spiritual and make room for other things – family, charity, reflection, even prayer and are able to put things into context make the more inspiring leaders." (Robinson, 2008)

"Business ethics is disorientated where workplaces deny spirituality, but more genuinely ethical when they nurture spirituality." (Moe-Lobeda, 2002. Healing a Broken World)

The 'hard' benefits

• Fulfilling obligations e.g. human rights; anti-discrimination.

+ Improving performance: research universally shows that organisations able to inspire employee loyalty to a higher 'cause' substantially out-perform their peers because of improved motivation, allegiance and commitment.

+ Spirituality positively affects employee and organisational performance by enhancing intuitive abilities and individual capacity for innovation, as well as increasing employee commitment. (Neck & Milliman, 1994)

+ Soul-friendly companies have below-average rates of absenteeism, sickness and staff turnover. (Lamont, 2002)

+ Zohar & Marshall (2004) claim that for every 1% improvement in staff retention companies get through their ethical trading stance, it adds $100,000 to their business bottom line.

The 'soft' benefits

+ Winning the war for talent: ethically-committed organisations have increasing appeal to particularly a younger generation, whose services are in great demand.

+ Releasing creative potential: organisations that encourage staff to bring their 'whole person' to work (body, mind & spirit) see benefits in creativity/ innovation and ethically-robust cultures reflected in corporate governance, corporate (social) responsibility and collective consciousness.

+ Nearly 75% of UK workers claim they would be interested in learning to live the spiritual side of their values, but 90% of UK managers believe their organisations have not attempted to discuss the issue of spirituality with their employees. (Howard & Welbourn, 2004)

+ Other benefits accrue through such characteristics as abundance, authenticity, compassion, discernment, forgiveness, freedom, honesty, gratitude, healing, humility, integrity, interconnectedness, meaning-making, mission, nurturing, peace, sense-making, service, stature, stillness, transformation, trust, vision, wisdom, honesty, integrity, authenticity, compassionate, wise, humble, committed to helping others etc. They move people – emotionally, physically and mentally, whilst role-modelling; they PULL, but not towards themselves so much as to something greater 'out there'. That is to say, they are emotionally-aware, have a strategic overview awareness of the impact of their attitudes and actions on those around them in the organisation but also in the community and the interconnectedness that might ultimately be global. Moreover, they seek the highest ethical standards and the greatest good for the greatest number. They are likely to describe or consider this as their mission, their contribution or payback to the world. Small wonder that leaders who possess these characteristics, habits and behaviours make a success of what they do – most organisations would pay a premium to employ people like them. Or, to put it another way, the characteristics that define and set apart leaders who have a high SQ are those highly sought-after by organisations.

On a similar theme *Management Today* magazine reported that: "*a desire to find a job with more meaning is a more common cause for exit than the pursuit of a fatter pay packet. Four out of five people say that 'making the world a better place' through their work was very important or absolutely essential to them.*" (Aug 2006)

CHAPTER 8

For more information on the **Conscious Capitalism** movement that Neal Gandhi referred to in his case study see: www.consciouscapitalism.org/node/3998.

In brief 'Conscious Capitalism' has four pillars guiding and underlying a business, detailed below. Of particular relevance to this book is the first of those pillars:

Higher Purpose: Recognising that every business has a purpose that includes, but is more than, making money. By focusing on its Higher Purpose, a business inspires, engages and energises its stakeholders.

Stakeholder Orientation: Recognising the interdependent nature of life and the human foundations of business, a business needs to create value with and for its various stakeholders (customers, employees, vendors, investors, communities, etc). Like the life-forms in an ecosystem, healthy stakeholders lead to a healthy business system.

Conscious Leadership: Human social organisations are created and guided by leaders – people who see a path and inspire others to travel along the path. Conscious Leaders understand and embrace the Higher Purpose of business and focus on creating value for and harmonising the interests of the business stakeholders. They recognise the integral role of culture and purposefully cultivate Conscious Culture.

Conscious Culture: This is the ethos – the values, principles, practices – underlying the social fabric of a business, which permeates the atmosphere of a business and connects the stakeholders to each other and to the purpose, people and processes that comprise the company.

Investing in the Future Generations

In the main text of the book I made numerous references to Millennials. They often share the characteristics of these calling to make a difference far earlier in life than Baby Boomers or even Gen X or Y.

For many people, making a difference or leaving a legacy is defined in terms of impact on the next generations. There are some interesting characteristics of the emerging generation of Millennials that suggest they may embrace the changes described in this book much earlier than the current Generation of Baby Boomers. (If this is not part of your consideration then do feel free to skip on to the next section below.)

Every generation likes to feel that it is unique. It likes to feel it will not repeat the mistakes of the past, especially those of their parents' generation, but will build something better, brighter and more robust. Millennials are no different to any other generation in this respect. But, Millennials (those born in the last decade of the 20th century and first decade of the 21st and therefore currently entering employment) face a number of unique challenges. They are the first generation perhaps ever to face the prospect of being materially less well-off than their parents. They face more employment competition from workers of other countries. And for a host of reasons may also suffer less good health and a reduced lifespan. Those whose legacy includes mentoring or working alongside Millennials soon discover that they are much more values-driven than Gen X, Y or even Baby Boomers in the Elder phase. They actively select businesses that they perceive as being ethically motivated towards their community, their clients and their staff. And they are very willing to leave if the company doesn't seem to live those values. They also want and expect to contribute, to be appreciated and to leave work with a sense of achievement.

They expect to be treated well. That not only means being treated with respect, honesty and generosity but also that their health needs will be covered (they suffer high levels of mental and emotional problems – more important to them at this stage than the physical side of wellbeing). Many of them have been brought up in families that are unstructured and fluid with little sense of permanence but where they have perhaps been central; they can struggle with the transition into the world of work, which can seem rigid, inflexible and impersonal. Sjors Bos, MD of I Heart Studios argues that this leaves them confused and questioning what they want out of life and who they are, much earlier than previous generations – who perhaps began from a firmer identity base in a more static society. (Quoted in an interview for The Academy for Chief Executives and available via **www.chiefexecutive.com/blog/case-study-motivating-millennials.**) He also feels that 'Just becoming self-sustaining is more of a challenge today: buying a house is a huge issue and so there's a certain level of angst which they have to deal with, and I don't think there is much of a support structure for that. Some of them worry that if they don't figure out who they are and what they want out of life that they'll get into a cycle of working just to pay the bills and find themselves stuck in a chain of cause and effect.'

My own observations suggest they have more sense of immediacy and individualism. They have been brought up to expect immediate gratification and see no reason why that should be any different at work. However, providing there is some form of short-term recognition of their contribution (praise, thanks, office applause) they are willing to forego the financial reward 'for a long time' (i.e. what they define as six months or more). Their average stay in a job is about two years before they expect to move on. And moving on may mean to a competitor; but it may equally mean into another sector altogether; it may mean into further full time skills-based learning; or even out for an extended career break.

Perhaps most significantly, and underpinning all of this, is their need for a sense of belonging. The last decade of their life, their formative years, has been full of uncertainty and lack of structure; fluid but also dynamic, so anything that smacks of formality or rigidity can be a problem to them. They want a sense of self-worth: they have been brought up to register the importance of feelings and so many of them are no longer prepared to look for just any old job or one with a long-term career structure. They want one where 'I can feel good and can contribute' – to both the business and the wider community.

ADDITIONAL RESOURCES

Out of many, two resources are of particular relevance to the themes in this book.

In the United States, *encore* (**www.encore.org**) is working to "build a movement to tap the skills and experience of those in midlife and beyond to improve communities and the world". They focus on leveraging the experience of older adults to improve our world now and for future generations by finding work that matters and makes a difference in the second half of life. Interestingly storytelling has been one of their key resources for changing perceptions of aging, contribution and value. Although *encore* appears to work primarily in transitioning highly experienced individuals into social purpose organisations and community enterprises, it also conducts research and runs Conferences, Fellowships and an annual Purpose Prize.

In the UK, PRIME (the Prince's Initiative for Mature Enterprise) concentrates on employment opportunities for those over 50 years of age. It recently merged with Business in the Community and is focussed on, 'Enabling older people to contribute their skills and talent through enterprise and employment'. Find out more via **www.bitc.org.uk/news-events/ news/prince's-initiative-mature-enterprise-merges-busi- ness-community**

BIBLIOGRAPHY

Booker, Christopher. (2004). *The Seven Basic Plots*. New York. Continuum.

Boyd, William. (2011). *Writers' & Artists' Yearbook 2012*. London. Bloomsbury.

Brehony, Kathleen A. (1996) *Awakening at Midlife – a guide to reviving your spirit, recreating your life and returning to your truest self*. New York. Riverhead Books.

Campbell, Joseph. (1993). *The Hero with a Thousand Faces*. London. Fontana Press.

Coelho, Paulo. *Eleven Minutes*. (2003) London. HarperCollins, p142

Covey, S. R. (2004). *The 8th Habit – from Effectiveness to Greatness*. New York. Free Press.

Denning, Stephen. (2005). *The Leader's Guide to Storytelling – mastering the art and discipline of business narrative*. San Francisco. Jossey-Bass.

Eliot, T.S. (1974) *Collected Poems 1909-1962*. London. Faber and Faber.

Goleman, D. (1995). *Emotional Intelligence – why it can matter more than IQ*. New York. Bantam Dell (Random).

Goleman, D. Boyatzis R., & McKee, A. (2002). *Primal Leadership: Realizing the Power of Emotional Intelligence.* Boston, Massachusetts. Harvard Business School Press.

Goleman, D. MacCoby, M. Davenport, T. Beck, J. C. Clampa, D. Watkins, M. (1998). *What Makes a Leader?* Harvard Business Review article, Massachusetts: Harvard Business School Press.

Haidt, Jonathan. (2006) *The Happiness Hypothesis: Putting Ancient Wisdom and Philosophy to the Test of Modern Science.* London. Arrow Books.

Hauge, Michael. (2011). *Writing Screenplays that Sell – the complete guide to turning story concepts into movie and television deals.* London. Methuen Drama.

Hopson, Barrie & Scally, Mike. (2008) *The Rainbow Years – the pluses of being 50+.* Middlesex University Press.

Horowitz, Ben. (2014) *The Hard Thing About Hard Things – building a business when there are no easy answers.* New York. HarperCollins.

Howard, Sue & Welbourn, David. (2004) *The spirit at work phenomenon.* London. Azure.

Ibarra, Herminia. *How to Stay Stuck in the Wrong Career.* HBR, (December 2002) Reprint R0212B

Ibarra, Herminia & Barbulescu, Roxana. *Identity as a Narrative: Prevalence of Effectiveness and Consequences of Narrative Identity Work in Macro Work Role Transitions.* Academy of Management Review, (2010), Vol 35, No 1, 135-154.

Ibarra, Herminia & Lineback, Kent. *What's Your Story?* HBR (January 2005). Reprint R0501F.

Isay, Dave. TED Talk: *Everyone around you has a story the world needs to hear.* StoryCorps. **www.ted.com/talks/dave_isay_everyone_ around_you_has_a_story_the_world_needs_to_hear**

Ismael, Salim. *Planning the Second Half of your Professional Life*. Web-based article, accessed August 2015 via **www.linkedin.com/pulse/ planning-second-half-your-professional-life-santiago-iniguez**

Kouzes, James M. & Posner, Barry Z. *The Leadership Challenge*. (2007). San Francisco. John Wiley & Sons.

Lamont, Georgeanne. (2002). *The Spirited Business*. London. Hodder & Stoughton.

Mackey, John & Sisodia, Raj. (2014). *Conscious Capitalism – liberating the heroic spirit* of business. Boston. Harvard Business Review Press.

McAdams, D.P. (2001). The Psychology of Life Stories. *Review of General Psychology*, 5, 100-122.

McAdams, DP. *Can personality change? Levels of stability and growth in personality across the life span*. In TF Heatherton & JL Weinberger (Eds), Can personality change? (299-313). Washington, DC.

Maslow, Abraham H. (1994). *The Farther Reaches of Human Nature*. Arkana Publishing. The Hierarchy appears in many different forms in many different publications. The official website is: **http://www.abraham-maslow.com/m_motivation/Hierarchy_ of_Needs.asp)**

Miller, William, **http://info.shine.com/Career-Advice-Articles/ Career-Advice/Can-spirituality-and-business-coexist/2777/cid2. aspx)** accessed 29th November, 2015.

Moe-Lobeda, Cynthia D. (2002) *Healing a Broken World*. Minneapolis. Fortress Press.

Nash, Laura & Stevenson, Howard. *Success That Lasts* HBR (Feb 2004) p102-109

Neck, C. P. & Milliman, J. F. 'Thought self-leadership: finding spiritual fulfilment in organizational life.' *Journal of Managerial Psychology*, 9 (6) 1994, p9-16

Palmer, Parker J. (2000). *Let Your Life Speak – listening for the voice of Vocation*. San Francisco. Jossey-Bass.

Peters, Dr Steve. (2012) *The Chimp Paradox – The Mind Management Programme for Confidence, Success and Happiness*. Vermilion.

Pollan, Michael. (1998). *Dream Pond – just add water. Then add more.* **http://michaelpollan.com/articles-archive/dream-pond-just-add-water-then-add-more/** Accessed August 2015. An article also appeared in **The New York Times o**n January 22nd, 1998.

Rooke, David & Torbert, William R. Seven *Transformations of Leadership*. Harvard Business Review. (April 2005) Reprint R0504D.

Seligman, Martin
www.authentichappiness.sas.upenn.edu/Default.aspx

Sheehy, Gail. (1997). *New Passages: Mapping Your Life Across Time*. London. HarperCollins.

Strenger, Carlo & Ruttenberg, Arie. *The Existential Necessity of Midlife Change*. HBR (Feb 2008). Reprint R0802E

Wigglesworth, C. & McElhenie, M. (2006). Validation Study for a Measure of Spiritual Intelligence. Conscious Pursuits Ltd.

Zohar & Marshall. (2004). *Spiritual Capital: Wealth We Can Live By*. San Francisco. Berrett-Koehler.

Thompson, C.M. (2000). The Congruent Life: following the inward path to fulfilling work and inspired leadership. San Francisco. Jossey-Bass.

Interviews by leadership expert Steve Tappin for the BBC's CEO Guru series, produced by Neil Koenig **www.bbc.co.uk/search?q=CEO%20Guru**

Lightning Source UK Ltd.
Milton Keynes UK
UKHW021908090220
358432UK00017B/391